总顾问：牛　健　丁国声
总主编：任静生

职场综合英语实训手册

（第二册）

主　编　张　荣
副主编　史雯娜
编　者　章素华　陈　婧　易雅琼
　　　　徐　萍　袁　平　黄海燕
　　　　吴　翔

图书在版编目(CIP)数据

职场综合英语实训手册(第二册)/张荣主编. —北京：北京大学出版社，2013.1
(全国职业技能英语系列教材)
ISBN 978-7-301-20800-7

Ⅰ. ①职… Ⅱ. ①张… Ⅲ. ①英语－高等职业教育－习题集 Ⅳ. ①H319.6

中国版本图书馆 CIP 数据核字(2012)第 127660 号

书　　　名：职场综合英语实训手册(第二册)
著作责任者：张　荣　主编
责 任 编 辑：郝妮娜
标 准 书 号：ISBN 978-7-301-20800-7/H · 3075
出 版 发 行：北京大学出版社
地　　　址：北京市海淀区成府路 205 号　100871
网　　　址：http://www.pup.cn　　新浪官方微博：@北京大学出版社
电 子 信 箱：zbing@pup.pku.edu.cn
电　　　话：邮购部 62752015　发行部 62750672　编辑部 62759634　出版部 62754962
印　刷　者：三河市博文印刷有限公司
经　销　者：新华书店
　　　　　　787 毫米×1092 毫米　16 开本　8 印张　230 千字
　　　　　　2013 年 1 月第 1 版　2015 年 11 月第 4 次印刷
定　　　价：25.00 元(附光盘)

未经许可，不得以任何方式复制或抄袭本书之部分或全部内容。
版权所有，侵权必究
举报电话：010-62752024　电子信箱：fd@pup.pku.edu.cn

前　言

　　《职场综合英语教程》是一套由西方文化入手，渐进涉及职场工作需要的高职英语教材。该教材遵循"以服务为宗旨，以就业为导向"的原则，结合高职英语教学的需要和高职学生的实际英语水平，具有较强的实用性和针对性。《职场综合英语实训手册》(第二册)(以下简称《实训手册》)，是《职场综合英语教程》(第二册)(以下简称《教程》)的辅助教程，内容与《教程》(第二册)有所兼顾，同时又充分考虑到"高等学校英语应用能力考试(B级)"(以下简称"B级考试")的实考题型，在结构上对"B级考试"的题型进行了套用。这样设计的目的有三：一、增强学生的动手能力，包括记录所听材料的关键词，写摘要，翻译英语语句，用英语写应用文等。二、通过练习检测学生学习《教程》(第二册)的效果，帮助教师了解学生学习中的困难，从而更有效地施教。三、帮助学生了解"B级考试"的要求，以便学生顺利通过这项旨在检测高职学生英语是否合格的等级考试。

　　《实训手册》(第二册)包含八个单元练习。所有练习均参照"B级考试"的题型和题数，并在内容上尽可能保持与《教程》(第二册)的单元内容一致。

　　在对《实训手册》(第二册)进行实际训练时，建议学生把重点放在做题方法上。比如，做"Vocabulary & Structure"的要点是发现题干中的关键词。

　　例题：

16. The report gives a _____ picture of the company's future development.
　　A. central　　B. clean　　C. clear　　D. comfortable

(2010年12月试卷)

做这一题的要点是把题干中的 picture 看作关键词。所给选项中 central 表示"中心的";clean 表示"清洁的";clear 表示"清晰的";comfortable 表示"舒服的"。只有 clear 与 picture 搭配最好;因此,属于最好选项。

再看一例:

26. Could you tell me the (different) _____ between American and British English in business writing?

(2010 年 12 月试卷)

本题的关键词是空白处前面的 tell。所填词显然应该是 tell 的宾语,different 是形容词,不能做宾语,应填 difference。

我们再以阅读理解为例。下面是 2010 年 12 月"B 级考试"的实考题:

MEMO

To: Katherine Anderson, Manager
From: Stephen Black, Sales Department
Date: 19 November, 2010
Subject: Resignation(辞职)

Dear Ms. Katherine Anderson,

I am writing to inform you of my intention to resign(辞职)from G&S Company.

I very much appreciate my four years' working for the company. The training has been excellent and I have gained valuable experience working within an efficient and friendly team environment. In particular, I am very grateful for your personal guidance during these first years of my career.

I feel now that it is time to further develop my knowledge and skills in a different environment.

I would like to leave, if possible, in a month's time on Saturday, 18 December. This will allow me to complete my current job responsibilities. I hope that this suggested arrangement is acceptable to the company.

Once again, thank you for your attention.

前言

Memo

Date: 19 November, 2010
Memo to: Katherine Anderson, (46) _____
Memo from: (47) _____, Sales Department
Subject: Resignation
Years of working for G&S Company: (48) _____
Reasons for leaving: to further develop (49) _____ in another environment
Time of leaving the position: on (50) _____

做类似题目的要点是带着题目在原文中找结构,而不是理解原文,因此,很多时候不需要对原文进行逐句阅读。

就上述题目而言,(46)的要点在于填空前面的词:Katherine Anderson;(47)的要点是填空后面的词:Sales Department;(48)的要点在于填空前面的词:G&S Company;(49)的要点在于填空前面的词:further develop;(50)的要点在于填空前面的词:Time 和 on。

根据以上线索不难发现,本题的答案是:(46) Manager;(47) Stephen Black;(48) four/4;(49) knowledge and skills;(50) Saturday, 18 December。

《实训手册》(第二册)由安徽高职外语教研会组织编写,主要编写人员为芜湖职业技术学院的张荣和史雯娜以及其他学校的骨干教师。在编写过程中我们参考了大量的文字资料,对这些有关资料的编者我们深表感谢。同时,我们也深深知道,尽管我们认真地对本教程进行了审阅,书中错误仍然在所难免。在此,我们诚恳希望各位教师和同学在使用本书的过程中把编写之错漏记下来反馈给我们,以便我们以后通过修订,使本书更臻于完善。

编者
2012 年 12 月

目 录

Unit 1　Job Hunting ……………………………………………………………… (1)
　　Part Ⅰ　Listening Comprehension ……………………………………………… (1)
　　Part Ⅱ　Dialogue ………………………………………………………………… (3)
　　Part Ⅲ　Vocabulary & Structure ………………………………………………… (4)
　　Part Ⅳ　Reading Comprehension ………………………………………………… (6)
　　Part Ⅴ　Translation ……………………………………………………………… (9)
　　Part Ⅵ　Writing …………………………………………………………………… (11)

Unit 2　Interesting Jobs ………………………………………………………… (12)
　　Part Ⅰ　Listening Comprehension ……………………………………………… (12)
　　Part Ⅱ　Dialogue ………………………………………………………………… (14)
　　Part Ⅲ　Vocabulary & Structure ………………………………………………… (15)
　　Part Ⅳ　Reading Comprehension ………………………………………………… (17)
　　Part Ⅴ　Translation ……………………………………………………………… (21)
　　Part Ⅵ　Writing …………………………………………………………………… (22)

Unit 3　Business on Campus …………………………………………………… (23)
　　Part Ⅰ　Listening Comprehension ……………………………………………… (23)
　　Part Ⅱ　Dialogue ………………………………………………………………… (25)
　　Part Ⅲ　Vocabulary & Structure ………………………………………………… (26)
　　Part Ⅳ　Reading Comprehension ………………………………………………… (27)
　　Part Ⅴ　Translation ……………………………………………………………… (32)
　　Part Ⅵ　Writing …………………………………………………………………… (33)

Unit 4	Customer Service		(35)
Part Ⅰ	Listening Comprehension		(35)
Part Ⅱ	Dialogue		(37)
Part Ⅲ	Vocabulary & Structure		(38)
Part Ⅳ	Reading Comprehension		(40)
Part Ⅴ	Translation		(44)
Part Ⅵ	Writing		(45)
Unit 5	Culture Shock		(46)
Part Ⅰ	Listening Comprehension		(46)
Part Ⅱ	Dialogue		(48)
Part Ⅲ	Vocabulary & Structure		(49)
Part Ⅳ	Reading Comprehension		(51)
Part Ⅴ	Translation		(55)
Part Ⅵ	Writing		(56)
Unit 6	Technology and Life		(57)
Part Ⅰ	Listening Comprehension		(57)
Part Ⅱ	Dialogue		(59)
Part Ⅲ	Vocabulary & Structure		(60)
Part Ⅳ	Reading Comprehension		(61)
Part Ⅴ	Translation		(66)
Part Ⅵ	Writing		(67)
Unit 7	Elite Entrepreneurs		(68)
Part Ⅰ	Listening Comprehension		(68)
Part Ⅱ	Dialogue		(70)
Part Ⅲ	Vocabulary & Structure		(71)
Part Ⅳ	Reading Comprehension		(73)
Part Ⅴ	Translation		(77)
Part Ⅵ	Writing		(79)
Unit 8	Failure and Success		(80)
Part Ⅰ	Listening Comprehension		(80)
Part Ⅱ	Dialogue		(82)

目 录

Part Ⅲ　　Vocabulary & Structure ……………………………………… (83)

Part Ⅳ　　Reading Comprehension …………………………………… (85)

Part Ⅴ　　Translation ………………………………………………… (89)

Part Ⅵ　　Writing ……………………………………………………… (90)

答案及听力材料 …………………………………………………………… (91)

Unit 1　Job Hunting

Part Ⅰ　Listening Comprehension

Section A

Directions: *There are 5 recorded questions in it. After each question, there is a pause. The questions will be spoken two times. When you hear a question, you should decide on the correct answer from the 4 choices marked A, B, C and D.*

1. A. Yes, I am.　　　　　　　　　　B. Yes, I do.
   C. I'm sorry.　　　　　　　　　　 D. It's my pleasure.
2. A. Please do.　　　　　　　　　　B. Not yet.
   C. Yes, I know.　　　　　　　　　D. Most of the time.
3. A. It's early.　　　　　　　　　　 B. Eight hours.
   C. Yes, I'd love to.　　　　　　　D. At half past eight.
4. A. Nothing serious.　　　　　　　B. No, thank you.
   C. Yes, I have.　　　　　　　　　D. It's terrible.
5. A. Yes, I often go.　　　　　　　 B. Yes, I do.
   C. No, not yet.　　　　　　　　　D. No, thanks.

Section B

Directions: *There are 5 recorded dialogues in it. After each dialogue, there is a recorded question. The dialogues and questions will be spoken only once. When you hear a question, you should decide on the correct answer from the 4 choices marked A, B, C and D.*

1. A. Warm. B. Cold.
   C. Hot. D. Wet.
2. A. Go to Beijing. B. Meet him tomorrow.
   C. Book a ticket. D. Buy a book.
3. A. He's serious. B. He's careless.
   C. He's kind. D. He's polite.
4. A. They will stay at home. B. They will he late.
   C. They won't go to the party. D. They won't be late.
5. A. She doesn't need his help. B. She doesn't like the man.
   C. She wants to work for the. man. D. She wants to ask for help.

Section C

Directions: *In this section you will hear a recorded short passage. The passage will be read three times. During the second reading, you are required to fill in the missing words or phrases according to what you hear. The third reading is for you to check your writing. Now the passage will begin.*

The world population today is about 6 billion. But only about 11 percent of the world's land is suitable for farming. However, the area of farmland is becoming smaller and smaller ___1___. So it will be difficult to feed so many mouths. There are several reasons why farmland is being ___2___. First, a lot of the land is being used for the ___3___ of houses. Secondly, some of the land has become wasteland because wind and ___4___ have removed the top soil. Thirdly, some of the land' has become too salty to ___5___. Therefore, a big problem that we face today is hunger.

Unit 1 Job Hunting

Part II Dialogue

Section A

Directions: *Complete the following conversation by making the best choice in the table below.*

Brent and Stella are standing in front of their cash register 1.

Brent: Sales have been really weak for the past six months.

Stella: I know. ___1___.

Brent: Are you thinking what I'm thinking?

Stella: Perhaps.

Brent: ___2___.

Stella: Yes, I hate to say it, but we need to file for bankruptcy.

Brent: ___3___.

Brent is on the phone with his lawyer, Jenny.

Jenny: Are you having a hard time with the business?

Brent: Yes, ___4___.

Jenny: I'm sorry to hear that. I'll do my best to help.

Brent: Is it a complex process?

Jenny: It's not too difficult. ___5___ and then go to a court hearing.

Brent: OK. I'll stop by your office this afternoon.

Jenny: Sounds good. ___6___.

A. I'll call the lawyer in the morning and tell her we are going under.

B. We ran out of money and had to close the store.

C. I can't even remember the last time we made a profit.

D. I think it's time to face the problem.

E. Come anytime after two o'clock.

F. All you have to do is to sign some papers

Section B

Directions: *The following are some ways of interview. Read the words spoken and then match them with the functions.*

A. What is your major? (   )

B. I don't try to lead people. I'd rather cooperate with everybody. (   )

C. I'm working in a small company where a further promotion is impossible. (   )

D. Have you ever been employed? (   )

E. Your operations are global, so I feel I can gain the most from working in this kind of environment. (   )

F. How do you spend your spare time? (   )

G. I'm a hard-working, persistent person. (   )

1. To introduce your personality.
2. To ask about your working experience.
3. To show the reason for choosing the company.
4. To introduce your strengths.
5. To ask about your education experience.
6. To explain the reason for quitting from the former company.
7. To ask about your interests.

Part Ⅲ Vocabulary & Structure

Section A

Directions: *Complete each statement by choosing the appropriate answer from the 4 choices marked A, B, C and D.*

1. His plane is due at 10 in Paris. Look, _____ plane is now at _____ airport.

   A. a / the   B. the / the   C. the / an   D. a / an

2. I forgot both of the _____.

   A. rooms numbers   B. room number
   C. rooms number   D. room numbers

3. We are going to play _____ tennis in _____ afternoon.

   A. the/ an   B. the/ the   C. an / the   D. X / the

Unit 1 Job Hunting

4. How often do you go to _____?

    A. the movies   B. the movie   C. movie   D. movies

5. That was the second time I _____ abroad.

    A. have been   B. had been   C. have had been   D. was

6. He _____ from Florida State University in 1990.

    A. has been graduated   B. has graduated
    C. graduated   D. was graduated

7. If I _____ rich, I will travel all over the world.

    A. will be   B. am   C. can be   D. was

8. The students _____ basketball energetically on the playground right now.

    A. played   B. were playing   C. are playing   D. have been playing

9. The patient _____ the hospital for two days.

    A. came   B. went to   C. has come   D. has been in

10. The furniture _____ the decoration very well.

    A. matches   B. match   C. is matching   D. are matching

Section B

Directions: *There are 10 incomplete statements here. You should fill in each blank with the proper form of the word given in brackets.*

1. I believe that International Olympic Committee has _____ (*name*) Beijing for the 2008 Olympic Games.

2. Your happiness depends partly on your _____ (*attitude*) towards life.

3. The doctor told him to _____ (*relax*) for a month before going to work.

4. We _____ (*apologize*) for inconvenience caused by the train's delay.

5. More often than not, weather forecast _____ (*wind up*) the evening news.

6. As long as I work hard, my dream of _____ (*admit*) to TsingHua university will come true.

7. I just can't help being _____ (*attempt*) to have a try in translating the book into Chinese.

8. Everyone, old or young, should _____ (*contribute*) his share in the struggle against pollution.

9. The new look of the city _____(leave) a very deep impression on those foreign visitors.

10. All the passengers were killed in the plane _____(crash).

Part Ⅳ Reading Comprehension

Task 1

Directions: *Read the following passage and make the correct choice.*

You know the effect calories (卡路里) have on your body. For each pound of weight that your body carries, it takes about 12 calories to keep it alive. If you weigh 150 pounds, you need about 1,800 calories per day to keep yourself alive. It is bad that if you eat more. If you eat more than 1,800 calories per day, the extra ones turn into fat. Let's say that you eat 2,000 calories per day. That extra 200 calories are going to turn into fat. Then you go on a diet (减肥) and you eat only 1,000 calories per day over the long run. The diet really takes the weight off. But the weight comes right back when you return to your "normal" eating pattern. The lighter you are, the fewer calories you need. There are only two ways to keep the weight off: Change your overall (全面的) eating pattern, or start exercising so that you "burn" the extra calories you take in. The best course of action is to put these two ways together.

1. What kink of effect do calories have on your body?
    A. They make you become fatter.
    B. They help to keep you alive.
    C. They make you become thinner.
    D. They change your eating habit.

2. If an old lady weigh 200 pounds. how many calories does she need each day?
    A. 1 800.   C. 1 500.
    B. 2 000.   D. 2 400.

3. You are considered to be "bad", because _____.
    A. you eat more than you need   B. you eat less than you need
    C. you are in light weight   D. you are in heavy weight

4. Your weight will come right back when _____.
    A. you go back to eating 2 000 calories per day

Unit 1　Job Hunting

B. you stop going in a diet and eat as usual

C. the diet did not take the weight off as you expected

D. you don't need as many calories as usual

5. The best way for you to keep the weight off is _____.

A. to eat as less as it is possible

B. to do exercise as much as possible

C. to eat less and do more exercise

D. to go on a diet when you become fat

Task 2

Directions*: The following is a list of terms frequently used in marketing services. After reading it, you are required to find the items equivalent to (与……等同) those given in Chinese in the table below.*

A — attractive appearance　　　B — choice materials

C — bright in color　　　　　　D — high in quality

E — durable in use　　　　　　F — elegant and graceful

G — easy to handle　　　　　　H — fashionable style

I — great varieties　　　　　　J — fine in workmanship

K — moderate price　　　　　　L — quality and quantity assured

M — strong packing　　　　　　N — sufficient supplies

O — timely delivery guaranteed　P — with a long standing reputation

Q — delicious in taste　　　　　R — superior performance

Example：(F) 典雅大方　　　(J) 工艺精湛

1. (　) 价格适中　　　　(　) 味道鲜美
2. (　) 选料考究　　　　(　) 款式新颖
3. (　) 性能优良　　　　(　) 货源充足
4. (　) 交货及时　　　　(　) 操作简便
5. (　) 经久耐用　　　　(　) 包装牢固

Task 3

Directions: *Complete the information by filling in the blanks. Write your answers in no more than 3 words.*

Rules of the Reading Room

Welcome to the library.

1) This reading room is specially for use of all students of this college.

2) Please keep quiet and keep the room neat and clean.

3) Do not talk or laugh loudly; do not smoke or eat; do not litter (乱扔) with waste paper and throw them into the waste basket.

4) Do not take any newspapers or magazines out of the reading room.

5) Produce your student card or ID (identity card) when borrowing books. Borrow only one book at a time.

6) Protect public property. Do not scribble (乱涂) on the pages of books or tear them out. Any damage done will be fined.

7) Do not move the desks or chairs about.

8) For any information in relation to the library, please contact the librarian.

The library of Yingcai Technology College

April 1, 2005

1. Who can use this reading room?
   _____ of this college.
2. What should a student do if he or she wants to borrow books from the library?
   They should first produce their _____ or ID.
3. What are not allowed to be taken out of the reading room? _____.
4. What will happen if any student does damage to a book?
   The student will _____.
5. Whom should a student go to if he or she has any questions? _____.

Unit 1 Job Hunting

Task 4

Directions: *Complete the answers that follow the questions in no more than 3 words.*

Yanton Playingfield Committee
Grounds-person(场地管理员)Wanted

The Yanton Playingfield Committee has for many years been fortunate to have Eddie Christiansen as grounds-person at its sports ground in Littlemarsh. However, after 10 years of service, Eddie has decided it's time to retire in July. The committee wishes him the best for his retired life.

However, this leaves us needing a new grounds-person. This role is part-time, averaging around 5 hours per week. The duties involve the mowing(除草), rolling, and trimming(修剪)of the field edges. Applicants(求职者)need to be able to drive and use the equipment needed for the above-mentioned duties.

Applicants can either contact Hugh Morris, 42 Spencer Avenue, tel. 765-4943780, to discuss or register an interest in the position, or any member of the Playingfield Committee.

1. Which organization is in need of a grounds-person?
   The _____.
2. Why is a new grounds-person needed?
   Because the former grounds-person, Eddie Christiansen, has decided it's time to _____.
3. What are the duties of a grounds-person?
   His duties involve the mowing, _____ of the field edges.
4. What should applicants be able to do?
   They should be able to _____ the equipment needed for the duties.
5. Who is the contact person?
   _____ or any committee member.

Part Ⅴ   Translation

Directions: *This part is to test your ability to translate English into Chinese. Make* *the best choice and write the translation of the paragraph.*

1. They so behaved in the debate that we find it difficult not to admire them.

   A. 他们在辩论中如此表现了一番，以至我们不得不称赞他们。

   B. 他们在辩论中表现非常出色，我们很难不佩服他们。

   C. 他们在辩论中行为得体，使我们觉得难以超越他们。

   D. 他们在辩论中表现很糟糕，我们很难不为他们难过。

2. The successful completion of the book is the cooperation and confidence of many people.

   A. 本书的写作很成功，是因为许多人互相合作、具有信心。

   B. 成功地完成本书的写作是许多人互相合作、坚信不疑的结果。

   C. 这本书成功了，结果使许多人更加合作，更加信任。

   D. 许多人的合作和信任导致了这本书的成功。

3. Seldom can people find international news on the front page of this popular local newspaper.

   A. 人们不会在这份地方报纸前几页上寻找重要的国际新闻。

   B. 人们很难在当地这份深受欢迎的报纸头版看到国际新闻。

   C. 人们从这份当地发行的报纸第一页上几乎找不到国际新闻。

   D. 人们阅读当地发行的报刊时从不查看头版刊登的国际新闻。

4. It is reported that output is now six times what it was before liberation.

   A. 据报道，解放前的产量是现在的6倍。

   B. 据报道，现在的的产量是解放前6倍。

   C. 有人报道说，解放前的产量是现在的6倍。

   D. 有人报道说，现在的产量是解放前6倍。

5. The new Holiday Inn has everything you need for a weekend of family fun or business travel. Conveniently located, the Holiday Inn is within walking distance to the hot springs and the downtown shopping area. Each room has a refrigerator, coffee maker, and hair dryer. Guests will enjoy the Holiday Inn's swimming pool, as well as a free Western or Chinese breakfast every morning.

Unit 1 Job Hunting

Part Ⅵ Writing

Directions：*This part is to test your ability to do practical writing. You are allowed 30 minutes to write a letter. Suppose you are Mary. Write a letter to a friend of yours who send you a dictionary. You should write at least 120 words according to the suggestion given below in Chinese.*

1. 感谢他昨天送给你的英语字典；
2. 你一直想要这样一本字典；
3. 每当用到这本字典的时候,你都会想到他。

Unit 2　Interesting Jobs

Part Ⅰ　Listening Comprehension

Section A

Directions : *There are 5 recorded questions in it. After each question, there is a pause. The questions will be spoken two times. When you hear a question, you should decide on the correct answer from the 4 choices marked A, B, C and D.*

1. A. Thank you.　　　　　　　　B. With pleasure.
   C. Oh, yes.　　　　　　　　　　D. Here you are.
2. A. From 9 a.m. to 6 p.m.　　　　B. Far from here.
   C. Five people.　　　　　　　　D. One hundred dollars.
3. A. Please sit down.　　　　　　B. Take it easy.
   C. I'm OK　　　　　　　　　　D. Yes, of course.
4. A. He's a nice person.　　　　　B. I work very hard.
   C. You're welcome.　　　　　　D. Certainly not.
5. A. It's far away.　　　　　　　B. It's rather warm.
   C. I hope so.　　　　　　　　　D. I'm afraid I can't.

Unit 2 Interesting Jobs

Section B

Directions: *There are 5 recorded dialogues in it. After each dialogue, there is a recorded question. The dialogues and questions will be spoken only once. When you hear a question, you should decide on the correct answer from the 4 choices marked A, B, C and D.*

1. A. From his friend.   B. From his teacher.
   C. From his boss.   D. From his brother.
2. A. Attend a meeting.   B. Hold a party.
   C. Take an interview.   D. Meet a friend.
3. A. In the meeting room.   B. In her office.
   C. At home.   D. At the bank.
4. A. It's very boring.   B. That's too busy.
   C. She likes it very much.   D. She's going to give it up.
5. A. An engineer.   B. A doctor.
   C. A salesman.   D. A secretary.

Section C

Directions: *In this section you will hear a recorded short passage. The passage will be read three times. During the second reading, you are required to fill in the missing words or phrases according to what you hear. The third reading is for you to check your writing. Now the passage will begin.*

People visit other countries for many reasons. Some travel ____1____; others travel to visit interesting places. Whenever you go, for whatever reason, it is important to be ____2____. A touist can draw a lot of attention from local people. Although most of the people you meet are friendly and welcoming, sometimes there are dangers. ____3____, your money or passport might be stolen. Just as in your home country, do not expect everyone you meet to be friendly and ____4____. It is important to prepare your trip in advance, and ____5____ be careful while you are traveling.

Part Ⅱ Dialogue

Section A

Directions: *Complete the following conversation by making the best choice in the table below.*

W: ___1___.

M: My name is David and I live in Shanghai, I was born in 1980. My major was electrical engineering.

W: ___2___.

M: Well, I approach things very enthusiastically, I think, and I don't like to leave things half-done. ___3___.

W: What would you say are your weaknesses and strengths?

M: Well, I'm afraid I'm a poor speaker, however I'm fully aware of this, so I've been studying how to speak in public. ___4___.

W: ___5___.

M: I have a driver's license, and I am a CPA (Certified Public Accountant).

W: How do you relate to others?

M: ___6___.

> A. I'm very organized and extremely capable.
> B. Do you have any licenses or certificates?
> C. Tell me a little bit about yourself.
> D. I'm very co-operative and have good teamwork spirit.
> E. What kind of personality do you think you have?
> F. I suppose my strengths are I'm persistent and a fast-learner.

Section B

Directions: *The following are some ways of greeting and bidding farewell. Read*

Unit 2 Interesting Jobs

the words spoken and then match them with the functions.

A. I have worked for two years with an American Company. (   )

B. I hope you'll consider my experience and training and will offer me a salary higher than the junior secretary's salary. (   )

C. What made you decide to change your job? (   )

D. How long does it take to get here from your home? (   )

E. Do you have allowance for transportation as well a housing packages? (   )

F. If you enter this company, what section would you like to work in? (   )

G. What are your salary expectations? (   )

1. To ask about the reason for job changing.
2. To ask about your requirements on income.
3. To ask about the benefit of the company.
4. To show the working experience.
5. To ask for the related salary.
6. To ask about the ideal department.
7. To ask about the distance between your house and the company.

Part Ⅲ　Vocabulary & Structure

Section A

Directions: *Complete each statement by choosing the appropriate answer from the 4 choices marked A, B, C and D.*

1. It is reported that cigarettes made in USA _____ better abroad, especially in Asia.

   A. are sold　　　B. sold　　　C. were selling　　　D. sell

2. What _____ to her will probably remain a secret for ever.

   A. took place　　　　　　B. was taken place

   C. happened　　　　　　D. was happened

3. I prefer to live in the country rather than _____ in a city.

   A. to live　　　B. live　　　C. living　　　D. lived

4. Mr. John's monthly income has increased _____ 900 dollars.
   A. in   B. at   C. by   D) on

5. I wish I _____ to the play with you last Sunday.
   A. did go   B. went   C. had gone   D. have gone

6. He _____ Master's Degree in Literature last year.
   A. awarded   B. was awarded
   C. has been awarded   D. has awarded

7. The professor _____ the questions to the students already.
   A. explained   B. has explained
   C. is explaining   D. will explain

8. Linda burst into tears _____ she heard the bad news.
   A. the moment   B. soon after   C. at the time   D. every time

9. It was between 1830 and 1835 _____ the modern newspaper was born.
   A. when   B. that   C. which   D. because

10. She used to _____ in the middle school when she was young.
    A. teach   B. to teach   C. teaching   D. taught

Section B

Directions: *There are 10 incomplete statements here. You should fill in each blank with the proper form of the word given in brackets.*

1. After exchanging a few words about the weather, they _____ (*turn to*) business matters.

2. The teacher assigned us so much homework that almost every one of us felt _____ (*discourage*).

3. Li Ming is _____ (*on the way*) to Li Hong's home and she will talk with Li about the party held last night.

4. University graduates often find it hard to _____ (*apply*) what they have learnt at college to their jobs.

5. Cindy is beautiful, slim and tall. She is _____ (*promising*) to be a good fashion model.

6. Some famous Chinese poems are _____ (*explored*) in the dissertation pa-

Unit 2　Interesting Jobs

pers by overseas postgraduates.

7. As long as I work hard, my dream of _____ (admit) to TsingHua university will come true.

8. We are not well _____ (acquainted with) all the facts.

9. It's hard for me to express how much I _____ (appreciate) all your kind help and understanding.

10. The ages of the students _____ (vary) from 18 to 21.

Part Ⅳ　Reading Comprehension

Task 1

Directions: Read the following passage and make the correct choice.

In the United States, the fall holiday season begins on Thanksgiving Day, the fourth Thursday in November. Originally (最初) a day of thanks for good harvests, it is celebrated with a big dinner, and turkey (火鸡) is the traditional main course. Christmas comes on December 25, about a month after Thanksgiving. At Christmas time, people give each other gifts and send Christmas cards. Children especially look forward to this season. New Year' Eve, December 31, comes a week after Christmas. On New Year's Eve, people have gay parties to celebrate the end of the old year and the beginning of the new. This is the end of the holiday season. Easter comes in March or April. This is a religious holiday, and it also celebrates the coming of spring. At Easter, children receive gifts of baskets containing toy rabbits or chickens and eggs. On Easter Sunday, many people go to church. It is also a traditional time for woman to buy new clothes.

1. When does the fall holiday season begin in the United States?
   A. At Christmas.　　　　　　　B. On New Year's Eve.
   C. On Thanksgiving Day.　　　D. On Easter Sunday.

2. What do people do on Thanksgiving Day according to the passage?
   A. Grateful for good harvests.　B. Celebrate it with a big party.
   C. Eat turkeys　　　　　　　　D. Give each other gifts.

3. Why do children in the United States look forward to Christmas?

   A. Because they can eat turkeys.

   B. Because they can wear new clothes.

   C. Because they have a good holiday.

   D. Because they can receive gifts and send cards.

4. New Year's Eve means the end of the old year, the beginning of the new, and _____.

   A. the coming of spring

   B. the end of the holiday season

   C. the beginning of giving big parties

   D. the time for women to buy their new clothes

5. On Easter Sunday, many American people will _____.

   A. visit friends   B. go to church

   C. have dinner parties   D. send cards to each other

Task 2

Directions: *The following is a list of terms frequently used in abbreviated form. After reading it, you are required to find the items equivalent to（与……等同）those given in Chinese in the table below.*

A — CBO (Chief Business Officer)

B — CDO (Chief Development Officer)

C — CEO (Chief Executive Officer)

D — CFO (Chief Finance Officer)

E — CHRO (Chief Human Resource Officer)

F — CIO (Chief Information Officer)

G — CMO (Chief Marketing Officer)

H — CNO (Chief Negotiation Officer)

I — COO (Chief Operation Officer)

J — CPRO (Chief Public Relation Officer)

K — CQCO (Chief Quality Control Officer)

L — CRO (Chief Research Officer)

Unit 2 Interesting Jobs

M — CSO (Chief Sales Officer)
N — CTO (Chief Technology Officer)
O — CUO (Chief User Officer)
P — CVO (Chief Valuation Officer)

Example:（C）首席执行官　　　　　　（M）销售总监

1. （　）质控总监　　　　（　）首席技术官
2. （　）首席谈判代表　　（　）开发总监
3. （　）研究总监　　　　（　）财务总监
4. （　）市场总监　　　　（　）评估总监
5. （　）首席营运官　　　（　）公关总监

Task 3

Directions：*Complete the information by filling in the blanks. Write your answers in no more than 3 words.*

　　How many coins have you got in your pocket right now? Three? Two? Or one? With a phone card you can make up to 200 calls without any change at all.

　　What do you do with it?

　　Go to a telephone box marked "phone-card". Put in your card, make your call and when you've finished, a screen tells you how much is left on your card.

　　It costs no extra for the cards, and the call costs 10 per unit, the same as any other payphone call.

　　You can buy them in units of 10, 20, 40, 100 or 200.

　　Near each Card-phone place you'll find a shop where you can buy one, They're at bus, train and city tube(地铁) stations.

　　At many universities, hospitals and clubs, restaurants and gas stations, on the highway and shopping centers. At airports and seaports.

　　Get a phone-card yourself and try it out.

An advertisement about Phone Card

The largest number of calls for one card: ____1____

Steps in making a phone call: 1) find a telephone box marked ____2____

                      2) ____3____ the card

                      3) make the ____4____

Where to buy a phone card: from a shop near a ____5____

Task 4

Directions*: Complete the answers that follow the questions in no more than 3 words.*

Problems	Probable causes	Suggested solutions
The display is showing the sign ":".	There has been a power interruption.	Reset(重新设置) the clock.
The fan seems to be running slower than usual.	The oven has been stored in a cold area.	The fan will run slower until the oven warms up to normal room temperature.
The display shows a time counting down but the oven is not cooking.	The oven door is not closed completely.	Close the door completely.
	You have set the controls as a kitchen timer(定时器).	Touch OFF/CANCEL to cancel the Minute Timer.
The turntable (转盘) will not turn.	The support is not operating correctly.	Check the turntable support is properly in place, and restart the oven.
The microwave oven will not run.	The door is not firmly closed.	Close the door firmly.
	You did not touch the button "START".	Touch the button "START".
	You did not follow directions exactly.	Follow the directions exactly.

1. What should you do if the display is showing the sign ":"?

    Reset _____.

2. What is the probable cause if the fan seems to be running slower than usual?

    The oven has been put in a _____.

Unit 2　Interesting Jobs

3. What are you advised to do if you have set the controls as a kitchen timer?

   Touch OFF/CANCEL to cancel the _____.

4. What is the cause for the turntable to fail to turn?

   _____ is not operating correctly.

5. What will happen if you do not touch the button "START"?

   The microwave oven _____.

Part Ⅴ　Translation

Directions: *This part is to test your ability to translate English into Chinese. Make the best choice and write the translation of the paragraph.*

1. The committee focused on the problems of the homeless, leaving other business until later.

   A. 委员会集中精力解决无家可归人群的问题,把其他事情放到日后处理。

   B. 委员会十分关注无家可归人群的问题,把其他人群的困难放到日后考虑。

   C. 董事会集中精力解决住房问题,把其他的业务推迟到日后再处理。

   D. 董事会面临着住房问题的困扰,致使其他的业务推迟到很迟才开展起来。

2. The New Times Company is an active as well as an improving company.

   A. 新时代公司是一家既有活力,又在不断进取的公司。

   B. 与其说新时代公司的业务活跃,不如说它得到了进一步的改进。

   C. 新时代公司虽然具有活力,但还需要进一步的改进。

   D. 如果说新时代公司充满了活力,那是因为它得到了进一步的改进。

3. Maybe you haven't noticed it in the market, but it is one of the five major health care tea drinks.

   A. 也许你从未在市场上见过它,可它却位居五大保健养生饮料茶之首。

   B. 也许你还没注意到这个市场,但这种茶饮料却有五种主要的保健养生功能。

   C. 也许你从未在市场上见过它,它却在五大保健养生饮料茶中占一席之地。

   D. 也许你还没注意到这个市场,但它却集中了五大保健养生饮料茶于一市。

4. After visiting all the rooms and halls, you may feel the old building is filled with historical glory.

   A. 看过内室,穿过厅堂,你会感觉到这幢古老的建筑散发着历史的魅力。

B. 看过内室后又看厅堂,你会感觉这幢破旧房屋有着光荣的历史。

C. 看过内室,穿过厅堂,你会感觉到历史赋予了你无尚的光荣。

D. 看过内室后又看厅堂,你会感觉到创造历史是光荣的任务。

5. Whether you have a large network or a small one, you know that the price of the computer is often only a small part of your total cost of using a computer. Administration and maintenance can drive up costs and affect performance. That's why we created a set of tools to help you use and manage your systems.

Part Ⅵ Writing

Directions: *This part is to test your ability to do practical writing. You are allowed 30 minutes to write a poster. You should write at least 120 words according to the suggestion given below in Chinese.*

篮球比赛

队伍:安徽大学 VS 安徽师范大学

时间:8:30 a.m. 11月4号(周四)

地点:学校操场

请联系学生会索票,3辆大巴将接观众去球场。

观众应在早上8点在图书馆门口集合。

Unit 3 Business on Campus

Part Ⅰ Listening Comprehension

Section A

Directions: *There are 5 recorded questions in it. After each question, there is a pause. The questions will be spoken two times. When you hear a question, you should decide on the correct answer from the 4 choices marked A, B, C and D.*

1. A. Look, just over there.
   B. The hospital is too small.
   C. There are two hospitals here.
   D. It's ten o'clock.

2. A. I like playing football.   B. I'd like to.
   C. I don't want to know.   D. I think so.

3. A. Thanks a lot.   B. Can I help you?
   C. What shall I do?   D. Here you are.

4. A. Thank you.
   B. This pair of shoes is wonderful.
   C. Go ahead, at the corner.
   D. For two days.

5. A. Thank you. B. I agree with you.
   C. Me, too. D. A little better.

Section B

Directions: *There are 5 recorded dialogues in it. After each dialogue, there is a recorded question. The dialogues and questions will be spoken only once. When you hear a question, you should decide on the correct answer from the 4 choices marked A, B, C and D. Then you should mark your choice.*

1. A. They don't have to go the concert.
   B. His brother will let them use the car.
   C. The subway is fine with her.
   D. They'll have to rent a car as early as possible.

2. A. 6:00 p.m. B. 8:00 p.m.
   C. 9:00 p.m. D. It is delayed.

3. A. 10 minutes. B. 15 days.
   C. 20 days. D. 60 minutes.

4. A. The man is concerned about the color choice.
   B. The man doesn't care which color is chosen.
   C. The woman has chosen a nice color.
   D. The man's choice is different from the woman's.

5. A. A waitress. B. A salesgirl.
   C. A housewife. D. A receptionist.

Section C

Directions: *In this section you will hear a recorded short passage. The passage will be read three times. During the second reading, you are required to fill in the missing words or phrases according to what you hear. The third reading is for you to check your writing. Now the passage will begin.*

What do we know about sea? Most of us have seen it. Many of us have swum in it. We know that it looks very pretty when the sun is shining on it. And we also know that

Unit 3 Business on Campus

the sea is full of waves. Waves are beautiful to look at, but they can ___1___ ships at sea, as well as houses and buildings near the shore. What causes waves? Most waves are caused by winds blowing over the ___2___ of the water. The sun heats the earth, causing the air to rise and the winds to blow. The winds blow across the sea, pushing little waves into enormous ones. When the wind is blowing at 120 ___3___ per hour, most waves will be about 12 meters high. In 1993 the United States ___4___ the largest measured wave in history. It rose in the Pacific Ocean to a ___5___ of 34 meters.

Part II Dialogue

Section A

Directions: *Complete the following conversation by making the best choice in the table below.*

Tom: Hello, Lucy! I've ___1___. Have you seen it anywhere?

Lucy: Sorry, I haven't. ___2___ ask Jim? Perhaps he's seen it.

Tom: Thanks, I will.

Lucy: Oh, ___3___.

Tom: Jim, have you seen my dictionary?

Jim: Yes, I have. I saw it on Lin Tao's desk about ___4___. It must still be there.

Tom: Thanks very much.

Jim: ___5___.

A. You're welcome.

B. five minutes ago

C. here he is

D. Why don't you

E. lost my dictionary

Section B

Directions: *The following are some ways of communications in traveling. Read the words spoken and then match them with the functions.*

A. On the first day, it will get to HK and visit some of the famous spots in HK. (　　)

B. Hello, I'd like to book a double room. (　　)

C. What's the best season to visit Beijing? (　　)

D. When and how many days you would like for the trip? (　　)

1. Ask about personal information.
2. Arrange accommodation.
3. Ask about the appropriate time to visit a place.
4. Talk about traveling program.

Part Ⅲ　Vocabulary & Structure

1. The teacher asked me _____.
   A. how old I was　　　　B. how old was I
   C. how old I am　　　　D. how old am I

2. My question is _____ will marry a poor man like me.
   A. who　　B. whom　　C. what　　D. that

3. Tell the taxi driver _____ you want to go.
   A. what　　B. which　　C. where　　D. who

4. If I _____ you, I would accept the job.
   A. was　　B. is　　C. am　　D. were

5. It is desired that this rule _____ by everyone working here.
   A. should obey　　　　B. should be obeyed
   C. should obeyed　　　D. should be obey

6. There are two reasons _____ I don't want to go out tonight.
   A. why　　B. whether　　C. how　　D. that

Unit 3 Business on Campus

7. I have explained everything _____ I can to you.
   A. what   B. which   C. when   D. that

8. Because there were no buses, _____ we had to walk home.
   A. so   B. but   C. /   D. although

9. No sooner had I got home _____ it began to rain.
   A. when   B. what   C. then   D. than

10. You'll be late _____ you leave at once.
    A. until   B. where   C. whether   D. unless

Section B

Directions: *There are 10 incomplete statements here. You should fill each blank with the proper form of the word given in brackets.*

1. Without friends, he felt _____ (*lone*) in the city he had just arrived in.

2. The place has _____ (*develop*) from a fishing port into a thriving tourist center.

3. Traffic jams often _____ (*present*) problem that are different to solve.

4. They decided to _____ (*merge*) the two small companies into one.

5. The company _____ (*announcement*) that it is not responsible for the pollution in the river.

6. _____ (*slow down*)—I can't follow you when you speak so fast!

7. Read the _____ (*instruct*) before you switch on the engine.

8. Free umbrellas are _____ (*available*) at the entrance of the hotel.

9. I believe it's a terribly crowed theatre, so you'd have to _____ (*book*) the seats.

10. The police _____ (*force*) to open the door.

Part IV   Reading Comprehension

Task 1

Directions: *Read the following passage and make the correct choice.*

Shopping for clothes is not the same experience for a man as it is for a woman. A man goes shopping because he needs something. His purpose is clear and decided in advance. He knows what he wants, and his objective is to find it and buy it; the price is in the second place for consideration (考虑).

All men simply walk into a shop and ask the assistant for what they want. If the shop has it, the salesman quickly produces it, and the man begins to try it at once. For a man, small problems may begin when the shop does not have what he wants, or does not have exactly what he wants. In that case, the salesman will try to sell the customer something else. Very often, he offers the nearest thing which he can produce.

Now how does a woman go about buying clothes? In almost every respect, she does so in the opposite way. Her shopping is not often based on need. She has never fully made up her mind of what she wants, and she is only "having a look round". She will still be satisfied even if she has bought nothing.

1. How does a man go shopping when he wants to buy something?

    A. He will often ask help from the shop assistant.

    B. He will look at it carefully and wait for a while.

    C. He has made a plan before he wants to buy it.

    D. He will discuss it with his wife and then buy it.

2. What is a man's attitude to the price of goods?

    A. He cares much about it.

    B. He pays little attention to it.

    C. He is often not sure of it.

    D. He likes to ask his wife's opinion.

3. What does a man do when he can't get exactly what he wants?

    A. He often looks round the shop.

    B. He will ask the shop assistant for advice.

    C. He will decide to buy something instead.

    D. He doesn't buy anything else.

4. What does a woman usually do when she is going to buy something?

    A. She never arranges a plan for what she is going to buy.

    B. She doesn't ask the shop assistant to help her.

Unit 3 Business on Campus

   C. She seldom asks about its price.

   D. She will not try it on in the shop.

5. What is this passage mainly about?

   A. Men's way of buying things.

   B. Women's attitude towards shop assistants.

   C. The difference between men and women in buying things.

   D. Men are better in choosing what they will buy.

Task 2

Directions: *The following are some expressions. After reading it, you are required to find the items equivalent to（与……等同）those given in Chinese in the table below.*

A — Mini USB PC Interface

B — Built-in Smart Media Card Slot for Additional Memory

C — Super Compact Slim Design

D — Built-in 32MB Flash Memory

E — Compatibility Requirements

F — Audio Output Type

G — Dot-Matrix LCD Display Song Title

H — Supported Digital Audio Formats

I — Operating System Compatibility

J — Portable MP3 Digital Audio Player

K — Connectivity Technology

L — Water-resistant Design

M — Production Line

N — Requires 1 AA Battery

O — Model

P — Digital Preset EQs

Example：(P) 数字预设均衡器   (I) 操作系统兼容

1. (   ) 便携式 MP3 数字放音机   (   ) 生产线
2. (   ) 微型 USB PC 机接口   (   ) 嵌入式 32 兆闪烁存储
3. (   ) 需要一节五号电池   (   ) 点阵液晶显示歌名
4. (   ) 声音输出模式   (   ) 型号
5. (   ) 连接技术   (   ) 防水设计

Task 3

***Directions**: The following is a NOTICE. After reading it, you are required to complete the outline below it. You should write your answers briefly (in no more than three words)*

Notice

Over the past month the Personnel Office has about the approval process for using the new "flex-tine" working schedule. In order to know how to take advantage of this system, please keep this notice in your records.

First, you must determine if you are eligible(条件适合) to use a flex-time schedule. The flex-time system is designed for those employees whose jobs do not require them to answer telephones or to be available to the public between the hours of 8:00 A.M. and 5:00 P.M. In addition, an employee must receive written permission from his or her department manager.

Then, you must submit a copy of Form FT, signed by your manager, to the Personnel Office.

The Personnel Office will notify you when approval is cleared; you may then begin your new schedule on the following Monday.

You may obtain copies of Form FT from Mary White in Room 129. If you have any questions, see your department manager—do not contact the Personnel Office directly.

Unit 3 Business on Campus

Flex Time Working Schedule

Users: employee suitable for using it

Application process:

1. get ___1___ and
2. ___2___ a copy of Form FT to the Personnel Office, and then
3. be notified by ___3___

Starting time: ___4___

Contact person if there are questions: the ___5___

Task 4

Directions: *Read the passage carefully. After reading it, you should give brief answers to the 5 questions.*

Better your English and customer service skills in a better career.

Join our fast expanding team and you will be involved in customer service activities for our customers at our Data Processing Center. It's a career opportunity where you can use and develop your language skills, your customer service skills and supervisory (监督) skills. Right now we are looking for:

Section Head, Correspondence

In this supervisory role, you will lead a small team to prepare written relies for customer enquiries and instructions according to our Company policies and guidelines. You will identify customers' needs to ensure high service standards.

You should hold a degree, preferably in English, with supervisory experience in the service-related field, ideally involved in customer correspondence. As a team leader and decision maker, you must possess excellent interpersonal and communication skills and be proficient in written and spoken English and Chinese.

In return, you will be offered an attractive salary and other benefits. If you are interested, please apply by sending your detailed resume, quoting (引用) reference number SHC/G003 with expected salary by e-mail to: careers51@hsbc.com.hk

Applicants who are not contacted within four weeks may consider their application unsuccessful.

1. What is the position wanted in the advertisement?

   Section head of _____.

2. What are the job's main responsibilities?

   To prepare written replies for customer questions and find out _____.

3. What's the other qualification needed apart from a degree in English?

   _____ in the service-related field.

4. What favorable terms are offered for the job?

   _____ and other benefits.

5. How long should applicants wait before they know the result?

   At most _____.

Part Ⅴ Translation

Directions: *This part is to test your ability to translate English into Chinese. Make the best choice and write the translation of the paragraph.*

1. Consumer goods are abundant of good quality and variety.

   A. 顾客的商品质量好、品种多、供应充足。

   B. 质量好、品种多的消费者所需要的商品供应充足。

   C. 消费者好的事情是充裕的、好品质的、种类多的。

   D. 质量好、品种多的消费品供应充足。

2. The applicants who had worked at a job would receive preference in getting the position over those who had not.

   A. 有经验的人将被优先录用。

   B. 工作过的申请人将优先于那些没有工作过的人被录用。

   C. 工作过的申请人将得到偏爱超过没有工作的人。

   D. 有过工作的人将比没有工作过的人优先选择职位。

3. Insurance is to be covered by the buyer.

   A. 保险是被买方办理的。

   B. 保险是被买方覆盖的。

Unit 3 Business on Campus

C. 保险将由买方办理。

D. 买方将处理保险事宜。

4. The words and phrases given in this textbook are those that are likely to be needed by every person.

   A. 人们有可能需要这本教科书,因为它词汇给得很多。

   B. 这本教科书里的词汇是每个人可能需要的。

   C. 这本教科书提供的单词和词组是人们必须要用的。

   D. 这本教科书提供的单词和词组是每个人有可能要用的。

5. Although the state (Hawaii) is located in the tropical zone, its climate is comfortable because of the ocean (the Pacific Ocean) currents that pass its shores and winds that below across the land from the northeast. The temperature usually remains close to the annual average of 24 degrees Centigrade.

Part Ⅵ Writing

Directions: *This part is to test your ability to do practical writing. You are required to complete the application form according to the instructions given in Chinese below.*

说明:请按照下面的中文提示,以中国学生王小明(男)的身份填写下列XXX大学入学申请表格。具体信息如下:

出生日期:1989年8月20日

联系地址:广州市中山路710号

联系电话:020-61006571

个人情况说明:本人毕业院校和目前就职情况,所要申请的专业,个人学习兴趣以及希望对方提供的信息等。

Application Form

Family name: _____   First name: _____

Date of Birth: _____   Nationality: _____

Sex: _____   Telephone number: _____

Address: _____

Please write about your educational background and work experience, the university and the major you want to apply and the information you want to know. (about 50 words)

_____
_____
_____

Unit 4　Customer Service

Part Ⅰ　Listening Comprehension

Section A

Directions: *There are 5 recorded questions in it. After each question, there is a pause. The questions will be spoken two times. When you hear a question, you should decide on the correct answer from the 4 choices marked A, B, C and D.*

1. A. It was raining.　　　　　　　　B. Never mind.
   C. I had left it behind.　　　　　　D. It's comfortable.
2. A. Bread with butter is my favorite.　B. I like butter with my bread.
   C. I like having some bread.　　　　D. Yes, just a little, please.
3. A. He always took off his jacket and threw it on the bed.
   B. He was having a rest at that time.
   C. He had a rest at that time.
   D. He went to Shanghai.
4. A. It's very good.　　　　　　　　B. No, I don't think so.
   C. It's a capital letter.　　　　　　D. Yes, it's the last part.
5. A. It's interesting.　　　　　　　　B. Nothing interesting in it.
   C. Yes, there is a bad news.　　　　D. It's so bad.

Section B

Directions: *There are 5 recorded dialogues in it. After each dialogue, there is a recorded question. The dialogues and questions will be spoken only once. When you hear a question, you should decide on the correct answer from the 4 choices marked A, B, C and D.*

1. A. To practice his English every day.
   B. To correct his sentences.
   C. To finish his homework on time.
   D. To use the new words in sentences.

2. A. He was seeing a doctor.
   B. He was visiting his mother in hospital.
   C. He was looking after his mother.
   D. He was visiting a nurse.

3. A. 5:25. B. 5:35. C. 5:30. D. 4:00.

4. A. The bus had broken down and will not arrive.
   B. The bus was in a terrible accident.
   C. The bus will probably arrive at 9:15.
   D. The bus may arrive tonight, but the man isn't sure.

5. A. 5minutes late.   B. 30minutes late.
   C. 35minutes late.   D. 25 minutes late.

Section C

Directions: *In this section you will hear a recorded short passage. The passage will be read three times. During the second reading, you are required to fill in the missing words or phrases according to what you hear. The third reading is for you to check your writing. Now the passage will begin.*

Since World War Two, especially in the last few decades of the 20th century, large groups of foreigners have come and settled in the United Sates. The __1__ is that many Americans speak a foreign language at home. Today, one in seven Americans speaks a language __2__ English. Spanish is the leading foreign language spoken by 17 million Americans. All together, 31.8 million Americans speak 329

Unit 4 Customer Service

foreign languages in the ___3___. That means there is an increase of 34 percent in foreign language usage since 1980. Asia languages are used by 14 percent of foreign language speakers. That ___4___ the new wave of immigrants from Asia countries ___5___ India, Japan, Korea and the Philippines. However, fewer European languages are heard in American families than before.

Part Ⅱ Dialogue

Section A

Directions: *Complete the following conversation by making the best choice in the table below.*

Leslie: How are you this afternoon?

Paul: Just fine. I looked over the catalog you gave me this morning, and I'd like to discuss prices on your computer speakers

Leslie: Very good. ___1___.

Paul: Let me see. I see that your listed price for the K-two-one model is ten US dollars. Do you offer ___2___?

Leslie: ___3___. We give a five percent discount for orders of a hundred or more.

Paul: What kind of discount could you give me if I were to ___4___ for six hundred units?

Leslie: On an order of six hundred, we can give you a discount of ten percent.

Paul: I'd like to go ahead and place an order for six hundred units.

Leslie: ___5___ I'll just fill out the purchase order and have you sign it.

1. Great!
2. Here is our price list.
3. place an order
4. We sure do.
5. quantity discount

Section B

Directions: *The following are some ways of making deal. Read the actual words spoken and then match them with the functions.*

A. We can offer you this in different levels of quality. (   )

B. Is there much of a difference in price? (   )

C. Is this going to satisfy your requirements? (   )

D. How many different models of this do you offer? (   )

E. Did the material work out well for you? (   )

1. Ask about the material thing.
2. To inquire the price.
3. To announce the demands.
4. To ask about the models.
5. To ask about the quality of the products.

Part Ⅲ Vocabulary & Structure

1. I can hardly imagine so pretty a girl like you _____ boxing.
   A. like   B. to like   C. liking   D. to have liked

2. The manager decided to give the job to _____ he believed had a strong sense of duty.
   A. whoever   B. whomever   C. who   D. those

3. In _____ old society many young women died by so strange and cruel _____ custom.
   A. / ; a   B. / ; the   C. the ; a   D. an ; a

4. I like football. —_____ my sister and me.
   A. So do   B. So are   C. So did   D. So it is with

5. This is such a wonderful film _____ we have never seen.
   A. that   B. as   C. which   D. what

6. I like coffee with nothing in it. What about you
   I prefer coffee _____ sugar.

Unit 4 Customer Service

      A. to   B. for   C. with   D. than

7. What have we said _____ her so unhappy

    A. makes   B. to make   C. made   D. had made

8. In order not to be found, I'll spend the night _____ in your room.

    A. locking   B. locked   C. to lock   D. lock

9. Lily, do you remember the boss in _____ company we worked during the summer holiday. He is coming to see us.

    A. whose   B. whom   C. who   D. where

10. _____ nice, the food was sold out soon.

    A. Tasted   B. Tasting   C. To taste   D. Being tasted

Section B

Directions: *There are 10 incomplete statements here. You should fill each blank with the proper form of the word given in brackets.*

1. Any public demonstration *on a large scale* should obtain the _____ (*permit*) of the city authorities.

2. A balanced diet provides enough _____ (*nutrition*) for your body.

3. A month ago he received a notice stating his application was _____ (*deny*).

4. To install the software, please double-click the setup _____ (*icon*).

5. The _____ (*invent*) of wheels was a milestones in the history of mankind.

6. Her answer _____ (*reveal*) her to be an innocent person

7. The girl whose left leg had been _____ (*remove*) is doing well with the artificial leg.

8. The speaker was rather hesitant and had to be _____ (*prompt*) occasionally by the chairman.

9. The flower _____ (*symbolize*) the poet's love.

10. All baby bottles and other utensils should be sterilized to *guard against* _____ (*infect*).

Part Ⅳ Reading Comprehension

Task 1

Directions: *Read the following passage and make the correct choice.*

December 22, 2004

Dear Ms. Lin,

By the end of 1997, I began to be an office worker in this company. Working as your assistant for the past five years has been genuinely rewarding experience. Under your direction I have grown as an administrator（管理人员）. And I am grateful that you have given me a practical education in business administration.

As you may know, I have always been eager to broaden my knowledge in business administration and have additional experience in this field. Now I have such an opportunity and thus, I submit my resignation（递交辞呈） from the position of your assistant, effective from the 31st this month; but I could stay a week or two longer if needed to help train my replacement.

I leave with only good memories of you and the other people with whom I worked. Thanks to all of you for a valuable help to my career.

Yours sincerely,

Vince Agsaway

1. Vince Agsaway wrote this letter so as to inform _____.

   A. that he is going to leave the company

   B. that he is going to report on December 31

   C. that he is applying for the job as an assistant

   D. that he is going to stay a week or two longer

2. Vince found his past 5 years' experience _____.

   A. practical   B. genuine   C. grateful   D. rewarding

3. In his letter, we come to know that all the following statements are true except.

   A. He has always wanted to have more payment.

   B. He wants to express thanks to all his fellow workers.

Unit 4 Customer Service

C. He has always wanted to have more experience in his career.

D. He has wished to learn something new in business administration.

4. If Ms Lin agrees, Vince will probably leave the company not later than _____.

   A. January 7   B. January 14   C. December 22   D. December 31

5. In the letter Vice thanks Ms Lin a lot as he thinks _____.

   A. Ms Lin will help him train his replacement

   B. Ms Lin will accept his resignation readily

   C. Ms Lin has offered him a practical education

   D. Ms Lin has helped him to find a new opportunity

Task 2

Directions: *The following is a list of terms frequently used in shipping services. After reading it, you are required to find the items equivalent to（与……等同） those given in Chinese in the table below.*

A — assembly line   B — packer
C — forklift   D — explosive materials
E — fire extinguisher   F — loading dock
G — machine operator   H — electrical hazard
I — conveyor belt   J — safety boots
K — shipping clerk   L — time card
M — warehouse   N — hard hat
O — earplug   P — hand truck
Q — safety earmuffs

Examples: (F) 装载码头   (K) 运务员

1. ( ) 易爆材料		( ) 安全耳罩
2. ( ) 二时卡		( ) 安全靴
3. ( ) 装配线		( ) 灭火器
4. ( ) 安全帽		( ) 手推车
5. ( ) 机器操作员		( ) 输送带

Task 3

Directions: *Complete the answers that follow the questions in no more than 3 words.*

Sakura Scholarships offer students the opportunity of taking part in a three-month Japanese language course in the city of Kyoto. The scholarship covers free accommodation, meals and tuition. Return air fares between their country of residence and Osaka are paid, and $1,000 pocket money is also provided.

To apply for one of these Scholarships, you should write a letter of about 300 words, describing your own educational career so far, and giving reasons why you think our education would benefit from participation in the Sakura Scholarship Scheme.

The closing date for application is February 1, 2009. Applicants who have been selected for the short list(入选名单) will receive the notice by March 31. The final selection will be made on the basis of interviews held during May.

Applications are open to all students, regardless of age, sex or nationality, and are also open to people who are not currently full-time students.

Please apply to Ms. Kyoto Matsumoto, Sakura Scholarship Scheme, Sakura Trading Co, 200 East Avenue, London E97PS.

Sakura Scholarships
Course offered: Japanese language
Items covered:
1. accommodation, meals and ___1___
2. ___2___ air fares
3. $1,000 ___3___
Content of application letter:
1. describing the applicant's ___4___ so far
2. giving reasons for taking the course
Deadline for application: ___5___

Unit 4 Customer Service

Task 4

Directions: *Complete the information by filling in the blanks. Write your answers in no more than 3 words.*

Dear Ms. Pascal,

I would appreciate very much an opportunity to meet with you and demonstrate how my unique experience and education could be of particular advantage to your company's future growth.

My practice last summer at Pascal Business Systems helped me focus on my academic and career goals. My fourteen weeks with your company involved sales support activities including preparing brochures and catalogs, coordinating trade shows, providing data and information to salespeople in the field, and interacting with customers.

During the past two semesters I have concentrated on developing my electronic publishing and business communication skills. I am confident that I Can improve the ways in which Pascal Business Systems provides support for field marketing representatives. This would include designing and maintaining an online catalog which could be coordinated with current inventories(库存清单).

I am available for an interview at your convenience and look forward to an opportunity to discuss ways to improve operations and communications with field locations and sales. Thank you for your kind consideration.

Sincerely,

Lourdes Santiago

1. How long did Lourdes Santiago work at Pascal Business System?

    _____.

2. What activities was he involved in when he had his practice in the company?

    A whole variety of _____.

3. What special skills did Lourdes Santiago develop during the past two semesters?

    He developed electronic publishing and _____.

4. What could he do to help support the field marketing representatives?

    By designing and maintaining _____.

5. What is the purpose of the letter?

   Lourdes Santiago writes the letter to ask for _____.

Part Ⅴ Translation

Directions：*This part is to test your ability to translate English into Chinese. Make the best choice and write the translation of the paragraph.*

1. He died at 57 of cancer on Aug. 7, 2000.

    A. 他在57岁时逝世,即2000年8月7日,因患癌症。

    B. 他因患癌症于2000年8月7日逝世,享年57岁。

    C. 他在57岁时逝世,因他于2000年8月7日患癌症。

    D. 他因癌症于2000年8月7日在57岁时逝世。

2. Miniature landscape gardeners are all artists in a way.

    A. 从某种意义上来说,搞盆景的人都是艺术家。

    B. 盆景园丁都是一个方面的艺术家。

    C. 从某一点上看,搞盆景的人都是搞艺术的。

    D. 从某种方法看,搞盆景的人都是艺术家。

3. New concept is wanted to solve water shortage.

    A. 新的观念想解决水资源匮乏。

    B. 我们想要新的观念来解决水资源匮乏。

    C. 解决水资源匮乏需要新观念。

    D. 解决水资源匮乏所需的新观念。

4. Now the people will pay three times as much as they used to pay for a house.

    A. 现在人们要买一幢房子的钱得比过去多三倍。

    B. 现在人们要买一幢房子的钱将是他们习惯花的钱的三倍。

    C. 现在人们要买一幢房子将是他们习惯花的钱的两倍。

    D. 现在人们要买一幢房子将比过去多付两倍的钱。

5. Flexible working hours were invented in Germany in the late 1960s, but reached Britain only in 1972. The system allows workers to start and finish

work whenever they want, with only two requirements. Firstly, all workers must be present for certain "key" times in a day, and secondly, all workers must work an agreed total number of hours per week.

Part Ⅵ Writing

Directions: *This part is to test your ability to do practical writing. You are required to write a letter of Inquiry(询价信) according to the information given in Chinese below.*

内容：我厂对贵公司生产的男女自行车及童车感兴趣，能否请贵公司寄一份产品目录表和价格表。我公司是武汉最大的经销商，并在十个地区设有分公司。如果贵厂的自行车质量令人满意，价格合理，我们将大量订货。

发信人：王刚（销售部经理）

Words for Reference：dealer 经销商

Unit 5　Culture Shock

Part Ⅰ　Listening Comprehension

Section A

Directions: *There are 5 recorded questions in it. After each question, there is a pause. The questions will be spoken two times. When you hear a question, you should decide on the correct answer from the 4 choices marked A, B, C and D.*

1. A. That's all night.　　　　　　　　B. No kidding.
   C. It's great, I had a good time.　　D. Don't mention it.
2. A. With pleasure.　　　　　　　　　B. I like it.
   C. I quite agree.　　　　　　　　　　D. Yes, by all means.
3. A. I don't know.　　　　　　　　　　B. Yes, I do.
   C. Never mid.　　　　　　　　　　　D. As you like.
4. A. Fine, thanks.　　　　　　　　　　B. No, thanks.
   C. Thanks a lot.　　　　　　　　　　D. Yes, I have.
5. A. Nothing much.　　　　　　　　　B. Nothing serious.
   C. Never again.　　　　　　　　　　D. Never mind.

Unit 5　Culture Shock

Section B

Directions: *There are 5 recorded dialogues in it. After each dialogue, there is a recorded question. The dialogues and questions will be spoken only once. When you hear a question, you should decide on the correct answer from the 4 choices marked A, B, C and D.*

1. A. At a restaurant. B. At a bus stop.
   C. In a store. D. At the Customs.
2. A. Computer engineer. B. Teacher.
   C. Patient. D. secretary.
3. A. On vacation. B. On business.
   C. Teaching Chinese. D. Interviewing.
   E. It's monotonous. F. She doesn't know.
4. A. They are going to the cinema. B. They are going to buy books.
   C. They are going shopping. D. They are going to the art exhibition.
5. A. Boss and secretary. B. Teacher and student.
   C. Customer and waitor. D. Patient and doctor.

Section C

Directions: *In this section you will hear a recorded short passage. The passage will be read three times. During the second reading, you are required to fill in the missing words or phrases according to what you hear. The third reading is for you to check your writing. Now the passage will begin.*

Hello, everybody! On behalf of the college, I'd like to express my warmest ____1____ to you. We do hope all our students will feel happy and pleasant here. We would be pleased to offer you ____2____ help to make your life here fruitful and colorful. Here you can find many convenient facilities for you to use, such as a ____3____, two libraries and an indoor playground. We also have four dinning halls ____4____ Chinese food and Western foods. Any suggestions for ____5____ our service are welcome. Thank you for your attention.

Part II Dialogue

Section A

Directions: *Complete the following conversation by making the best choice in the table below.*

A: Good morning. ___1___.

B: We'd like to buy some famous Chinese arts and crafts articles. ___2___.

A: There are various kinds of such articles in our shop, for example, porcelain, embroidery, cloisonné, wood engraving, and writing brush. ___3___.

B: They're all marvelous! We'll buy one china tea set, one tri-colored pottery, one wood engraving, and three Chinese embroidery shirts. ___4___.

A: Altogether 880 yuan. Let me wrap them up for you.

B: That's fine. Here is 900 yuan.

A: ___5___.

B: Thank you.

A: Wish you have a good time in China.

A. What would you like to recommend?

B. May I show you around?

C. Here are the change and the receipt.

D. Can I help you?

E. How much are they together?

Section B

Directions: *The following are some ways of greeting and bidding farewell. Read the words spoken and then match them with the functions.*

A. Excuse me, but aren't you Mr. Korsa? (   )

B. So, what brings you to this part of the world? (   )

Unit 5 Culture Shock

C. How about meeting at Business Center tomorrow morning at 10:00? (   )

D. That's great! It's very nice of you to invite me. (   )

E. I'd like some special local products here, what would you recommend? (   )

F. Marvelous! I've never expected such a splendid building! (   )

G. Can you tell me...er, what are your hours, please? (   )

1. Saying you are surprised to see someone.
2. Suggesting on when and where to meet.
3. To identify someone.
4. To express your surprise of seeing a building.
5. To ask for suggestion from someone.
6. To ask about the business hours.
7. To accept an invitation.

Part Ⅲ　Vocabulary & Structure

Section A

Directions: *Complete each statement by choosing the appropriate answer from the 4 choices marked A, B, C and D.*

1. Bats are surprisingly long lived creatures some _____ a life span of around 20 years.

   A. having   B. had   C. have   D. to have

2. One Friday, we were packing to leave for a weekend away _____ my daughter heard cries for help.

   A. after   B. while   C. since   D. when

3. Since people are fond of humor, it is as well in conversation as _____ else.

   A. anything   B. something   C. anywhere   D. somewhere

4. English is a language shared by several diverse cultures, each of _____ uses it somewhat differently.

   A. which   B. what   C. them   D. those

5. The professor could tell by the _____ look in Maria's eyes that she didn't understand a single word of his lecture.

   A. cold   B. blank   C. innocent   D. fresh

6. He decided that he would drive all the way home instead of _____ at a hotel for the night.

   A. putting down   B. putting off   C. putting on   D. putting up

7. My schedule is very _____ right now, but I'll try to fit you in.

   A. tight   B. short   C. regular   D. flexible

8. Anyway, I can't cheat him—it's against all my _____.

   A. emotions   B. principles   C. regulations   D. opinions

9. All visitors to this village _____ with kindness.

   A. treat   B. are treated   C. are treating   D. had been treated

10. _____ an important role in a new movie, Andy has a chance to become famous.

    A. Offer   B. Offering   C. Offered   D. To offer

Section B

Directions: *There are 10 incomplete statements here. You should fill each blank with the proper form of the word given in brackets.*

1. They divided themselves into three groups _____ (*accord*) to age.
2. We condemn his foolish _____ (*behave*).
3. I think your conduct is _____ (*disgrace*).
4. _____ (*Environment*) appeal to people to use less plastic bags.
5. These goods are becoming _____ (*increase*) high-end.
6. It is important for teachers _____ (*interact*) with students.
7. The department store is well _____ (*operate*).
8. It is better to be prepared than _____ (*prepare*).
9. Real life is not a _____ (*romance*) story.
10. Do you have two _____ (*connect*) double rooms?

Unit 5 Culture Shock

Part Ⅳ   Reading Comprehension

Task 1

***Directions**: Read the following passage and make the correct choice.*

The garden city was largely the invention of Ebenezer Howard (1850-1928). After immigrating form England to the USA, and an unsuccessful attempt to make a living as a farmer, he moved to Chicago, where he saw the reconstruction of the city after the disastrous fire of 1871. In those days, it was nicknamed "the Garden City", almost certainly the source of Howard's name for his later building plan of towns. Returning to London, Howard developed his design in the 1880s and 1890s, <u>drawing on</u> ideas that were popular at the time, but creating a unique combination of designs.

The nineteenth-century poor city was in many ways a terrible place, dirty and crowded; but it offered economic and social opportunities. At the same time, the British countryside was in fact equally unattractive: though it promised fresh air and nature, it suffered from agricultural depression(萧条) and it offered neither enough work and wages, nor much social life. Howard's idea was to combine the best of town and country in a new kind of settlement, the garden city. Howard's idea was that a group of people should set up a company, borrowing money to establish a garden city in the depressed countryside; far enough from existing cities to make sure that the land was bought at the bottom price.

Garden cities would provide a central public open space, radial avenues and connecting industries. They would be surrounded by a much larger area of green belt, also owned by the company, containing not merely farms but also some industrial institutions. As more and more people moved in, the garden city would reach its planned limit——Howard suggested 32,000 people; then, another would be started a short distance away. Thus, over time, there would develop a vast planned house collection, extending almost without limit; within it, each garden city would offer a wide rang of jobs and services, but each would also be connected to the others by a rapid transportation system, thus giving all the economic and social opportunities of a big city.

1. How did Howard get the name for his building plan of garden cities?

    A. Through his observation of the country life.

    B. Through the combination of different ideas.

    C. By taking other people's advice.

    D. By using the nickname of the reconstructed Chicago.

2. The underlined phrase "drawing on" in Paragraph 1 probably means _____.

    A. making use of   B. making comments on

    C. giving an explanation of   D. giving a description of

3. According to Howard, garden cities should be built _____.

    A. as far as possible from existing cities

    B. in the countryside where the land was cheap

    C. in the countryside where agriculture was developed

    D. near cities where employment opportunities already existed

4. What can we learn about garden cities from the last paragraph?

    A. Their number would continue to rise.

    B. Each one would continue to become larger.

    C. People would live and work in the same place.

    D. Each one would contain a certain type of business.

5. What could be the best title for the passage?

    A. City and Countryside   B. The Invention of the Garden City

    C. A New City in Chicago   D. A Famous Garden City in England

Task 2

Directions: *The following is a list of terms frequently used in train services. After reading it, you are required to find the items equivalent to（与……等同）those given in Chinese in the table below.*

A — Admission by invitation card only.   B — Children not admitted.

C — Closed during repairs.   D — Do not pluck flowers on fruit.

E — Danger, keep out!   F — No smoking.

G — Danger——thin ice!   H — Don't feed animals.

Unit 5 Culture Shock

I — Don't touch please.
K — Dogs not allowed.
M— Don't litter the beach.
O — Drive slowly.

J — Don't proceed across the rail.
L — Don't dump rubbish here.
N— Don't spit on ground.
P — Don't disturb.

Example：（O）车辆慢行　　　　　　（B）禁止儿童入场

1. （　）此处不准倒垃圾　　　　（　）不要随地吐痰
2. （　）请勿采摘花果　　　　　（　）不要跨越栏杆
3. （　）危险！请勿靠近　　　　（　）不要给动物喂食
4. （　）不准带狗入内　　　　　（　）不要乱扔果皮废纸
5. （　）请勿抚摸　　　　　　　（　）薄冰危险！

Task 3

Directions：*Complete the information by filling in the blanks. Write your answers in no more than 3 words.*

Make our Tourist Information Centre your first call when planning your visit to Qingdao. Our friendly team can provide a wide range of services to make your stay enjoyable and unforgettable. We can book your accommodation（住宿）, from a homely bed and breakfast to a four-star hotel. We can provide tickets for local events and we are booking agents（代理商）for National Express and other local coach companies.

In summer we organize our own various programmes of Coach Tours of Qingdao, plus regular walking tours around Qingdao, all guided by qualified guides. We also stock a wide range of maps and guidebooks plus quality gifts and souvenirs（纪念品）. We can help you with advice on what to see, where to go and how to get there.

We look forward to seeing you in Qingdao.

Tours of Qingdao

Tour Services Provider: ___1___.

Services Offered:

   II. booking accommodation

   III. providing tickets for ___2___.

   IV. booking tickets from National Express and other ___3___.

   V. Organizing Coach Tours and regular ___4___ in summer.

   VI. providing various maps, ___5___, gifts and souvenirs.

Task 4

Directions: *Complete the answers that follow the questions in no more than 3 words.*

I'm sure you all enjoyed that trip along the Grand Canyon and the Colorado River. It's quite amazing, isn't it.

The next stop on our tour is the Petrified(石化) Forest. This is a huge desert forest that is not exactly made of trees. You see, the trees are so old that they have fallen and have turned to stone. They look just like fallen logs, but they are no longer made of wood. Instead they are made of beautifully colored stone. It's unbelievable to see all of these fallen trees from a distance and then up close to see that they are really stone and not wood.

When we arrive at the Petrified Forest, please be sure to keep in mind that it is against the law to take any petrified wood out of the forest with you. You may think about picking just a tiny little piece, but please don't do it.

1. Who is probably delivering this talk? _____.
2. How many places have they just been? _____.
3. Where are they going to now? _____.
4. What are the fallen trees made of?

   The fallen trees are made of _____.
5. What does the speaker ask them not to do?

   Not to take any _____.

Unit 5　Culture Shock

Part Ⅴ　Translation

***Directions**: This part is to test your ability to translate English into Chinese. Make the best choice and write the translation of the paragraph.*

1. We are confident that will get rid of those difficulties since the government has agreed to give us some more help.

    A. 由于政府已经同意给予我们一些帮助,我们有信心克服那些困难。

    B. 自从政府同意给予我们帮助以来,我们才下了脱贫致富的决心。

    C. 政府同意给我们一些帮助,因此我们要下定决心直面困境。

    D. 我们有信心克服困难,争取政府同意给我们一些资助。

2. The road department apologized for any inconvenience caused while road improvements were in progress.

    A. 道路部门对道路改造期间所带来的不便表示歉意。

    B. 道路部门为修建道路可能引起的不便进行了解释。

    C. 道路部门辩解说,新近造成的麻烦是因道路正在改建。

    D. 道路部门对不断改建道路会造成的任何不便表示歉意。

3. For safety, all passengers are required to review this card and follow these instructions when needed.

    A. 为了安全,请各位乘客反复阅读本卡片,务必按照各项规定执行。

    B. 为了保险起见,请各位乘客务必阅读本卡片,并参照相关内容认真执行。

    C. 为了保险起见,要求所有乘客在需要时都能看到这张卡片及以下这些内容。

    D. 为了安全,要求所有乘客仔细阅读本卡片各项内容,必要时参照执行。

4. Passengers going to the airport by arranged buses must take the bus at the time and place as shown below.

    A. 搭乘专线前往机场的旅客,务必在下列指定的时间和地点乘车。

    B. 乘公共汽车去机场的旅客必须乘这路车,时间和地点安排如下。

    C. 经安排搭乘汽车去机场的旅客,应按指定的时间和地点上车。

    D. 机场即将为旅客安排汽车,请注意下列指定的上车时间和地点。

5. We are glad to welcome our Chinese friends to this special Business Training Program. Here, you will have a variety of activities and a chance to exchange ideas with each other. We hope that all of you will benefit a lot from this program. During your stay, please do not hesitate to speak to us with questions or concerns. We believe this will be an educational and enjoyable program.

Part Ⅵ Writing

Directions: *This part is to test your ability to do practical writing. You are allowed 30 minutes to write a letter. Suppose you are Mary. Write a letter to Lily, a friend of yours who is going to Hong Kong. You should write at least 120 words according to the suggestion given below in Chinese.*

1. 欢迎她来香港游玩；
2. 推荐她游玩迪斯尼乐园；
3. 提醒注意事项。

Unit 6　Technology and Life

Part Ⅰ　Listening Comprehension

Section A

Directions: *There are 5 recorded questions in it. After each question, there is a pause. The questions will be spoken two times. When you hear a question, you should decide on the correct answer from the 4 choices marked A, B, C and D.*

1. A. With pleasure.　　　　　　　B. That's great.
   C. What a pity!　　　　　　　　D. Please don't.
2. A. About 10 dollars.　　　　　　B. By 12 o'clock.
   C. In the photo shop.　　　　　　D. A moment ago.
3. A. Why not?　　　　　　　　　B. I see.
   C. I don't think so.　　　　　　　D. Go ahead.
4. A. Yes, please.　　　　　　　　B. No problem.
   C. Don't worry.　　　　　　　　D. Thank you.
5. A. What's there?　　　　　　　B. Can I help you?
   C. No trouble.　　　　　　　　　D. Thank you very much.

Section B

Directions: *There are 5 recorded dialogues in it. After each dialogue, there is a recorded question. The dialogues and questions will be spoken only once. When you hear a question, you should decide on the correct answer from the 4 choices marked A, B, C and D.*

1. A. The man will do everything.   B. The man needs a car.
   C. Alice offers to help.   D. Alice is quite busy.
2. A. They are free.   B. They are charged.
   C. They are expensive.   D. They are cheap.
3. A. Many people died in a fire.   B. Two persons were injured.
   C. There was a traffic accident.   D. There was an air crash.
4. A. Buy a train ticket for her.   B. Enjoy a concert with her.
   C. Go to the meeting with her.   D. Drive her to the railway station.
5. A. Where to have the meeting.   B. When to have the meeting.
   C. Who to attend the meeting.   D. What to discuss at the meeting.

Section C

Directions: *In this section you will hear a recorded short passage. The passage will be read three times. During the second reading, you are required to fill in the missing words or phrases according to what you hear. The third reading is for you to check your writing. Now the passage will begin.*

Modern technology has a big influence on our daily life. New devices are widely used today. For example, we have to ___1___ the Internet everyday. It is becoming more and more ___2___ to nearly everybody. Now it's time to think about how the Internet influence us, what ___3___ it has on our social behavior and what the future world will look like. The Internet has ___4___ changed our life, there is no doubt about that. I think that the Internet has changed our life in a ___5___ way.

Unit 6 Technology and Life

Part II Dialogue

Section A

Directions: *Complete the following conversation by making the best choice in the table below.*

Linda: Good morning! _____?

Jack: Yes, I want to borrow a book.

Linda: _____?

Jack: No, I don't have one now. _____?

Linda: Well, please fill in this form first.

Jack: OK. (A few minutes later.) here's the completed form.

Linda: Thanks. The card will be ready in thirty minutes, and you can take it later.

Jack: Thank you. By the way, _____?

Linda: Well, two weeks. But then, you can renew the book if you still need it.

Jack: I see. Thanks a lot.

Linda: _____.

A. How can I get one
B. What can I do for you
C. My pleasure
D. how long can I keep the book
E. Have you got a library card

Section B

Directions: *The following are some ways of communicating by phone. Read the words spoken and then match them with the functions.*

A. Is there any message I can give her? (   )

B. Hello, I'd like to speak to Ms Kim. (   )

C. Could I have extension 443? (   )

D. Would you mind telling Tom that I want to see him this afternoon? (   )

E. Hello, ABC Company. Can I help you? (   )

1. Extend a phone call.
2. Answering a phone.
3. Leaving a message.
4. Pass the message to the person called.
5. Make a phone call.

Part III Vocabulary & Structure

Section A

Directions: *Complete each statement by choosing the appropriate answer from the 4 choices marked A, B, C and D.*

1. It's the third time I _____ him this month
   A had seen   B. see   C. saw   D. have seen

2. They _____ a candle and the _____ candle _____ the room
   A. light, lighting, lit   B. lit, lighted, lit
   C. lit, lighting, lit   D. lighted, lit, lit

3. The grass will grow more quickly _____ regularly.
   A. if watering   B. if to water   C. watered   D. if watered

4. Last night a fire _____ in that market, so the firm suffered a heavy loss.
   A. broke up   B. broke out   C. broke off   D. broke down

5. When dealing with a _____ task, Alice always asks for help from people around her.
   A. difficult   B. wonderful   C. funny   D. simple

6. I got seriously ill and stayed in hospital last year and only then _____ the importance of health.
   A. had I realized   B. I had realized   C. realized I   D. did I realize

Unit 6 Technology and Life

7. Workers that have developed unique skills have _____ a lot of success either in jobs or in their own businesses.

   A. appreciated   B. enjoyed   C. finished   D. seized

8. My father did not go to New York; the doctor suggested that he _____ there.

   A. not went   B. won't go   C. not go   D. not to go

9. I love strawberries, but they don't _____ me.

   A. agree with   B. agree to   C. agree on   D. agree

10. You should take care that you have not _____ any detail in the design.

    A. disappeared   B. thrown   C. delivered   D. neglected

Section B

Directions: *There are 10 incomplete statements here. You should fill each blank with the proper form of the word given in brackets.*

1. She is the _____ (*dominate*) child in the group.
2. Several companies are _____ (*competent*) for the contract.
3. The National Theater _____ (*presentation*) 'Hamlet' in a new production.
4. We should respect a nation's territorial _____ (*integral*).
5. Fresh air is _____ (*benefit*) to one's health.
6. Her _____ (*active*) include tennis and painting.
7. He is _____ (*addition*) to TV soap operas.
8. Students are standing in a _____ (*encircle*).
9. She is a(n) _____ (*account*) of a large company.
10. We should _____ (*unit*) to fight against hunger.

Part Ⅳ Reading Comprehension

Task 1

Directions: *Read the following passage and make the correct choice.*

Some cities have planned their transportation systems for car owners. That is what Los Angeles did. Los Angeles decides to build highways for cars rather than spending money on public transportation.

This decision was suitable for Los Angeles. The city grew outward instead of upward. Los Angeles never built many tall apartment buildings. Instead, people live in houses with gardens.

In Los Angeles, most people drive cars to work. And every car has to have a parking space. So many buildings where people work also have parking lots.

Los Angeles also became a city without a Central Business District (CBD). If a city has a CBD, crowds of people rush into it every day to work. If people drive to work, they need lots of road space.

So Los Angeles developed several business districts and built homes and other buildings in between the districts. This required more roads and parking spaces.

Some people defend this growth patterns. They say Los Angeles is the city of the future.

1. According to the passage, Los Angeles is a city where _____.

    A. there is no public transportation system

    B. more money is spent on highways for cars

    C. more money is spent on public transportation system

    D. public transportation is more developed than in other cities

2. "The city grew outward instead of upward" means _____.

    A. the city became more spread out instead of growing taller

    B. there were fewer small houses than tall building

    C. rapid development to place in the city center

    D. many tall buildings could be found in the city

3. According to the passage, if a city has several business districts, _____.

    A. people won't have to drive to work everyday

    B. there have to be more roads and parking spaces

    C. companies would be located in between the districts

    D. there would be no need to build parking spaces within the districts

4. According to the growth pattern of Los Angeles, homes were mainly

Unit 6 Technology and Life

built _____.

A. in the city center B. along the main roads

C. around business districts D. within the business districts

5. The passage is mainly about _____.

A. the construction of parking spaces in Los Angeles

B. the new growth pattern of the city of Los Angeles

C. the public transportation system in Los Angeles

D. the location of the companies in Los Angeles

Task 2

Directions: *The following is a list of terms frequently used in cell phones. After reading it, you are required to find the items equivalent to (与……等同) those given in Chinese in the table below.*

A — phone book B — tools
C — calculator D — message saving
E — phone setting F — backlight setting
G — key lock H — automatic redial
I — sound volume J — ring type
K — voice mail L — additional functions
M — own number N — alarm
O — new message P — network
Q — delete all

Example:(C) 计算器   (K) 语音信箱

1. ( ) 自动重拨   ( ) 本机号码
2. ( ) 闹钟   ( ) 音量
3. ( ) 网络   ( ) 信息存储
4. ( ) 工具箱   ( ) 背景光设置
5. ( ) 电话簿   ( ) 话机设置

Task 3

Directions: *Complete the information by filling in the blanks. Write your answers in no more than 3 words.*

Hard Work, Good Money

We need:

    Staff to work in a busy operation centre.

    You to be working in Hangzhou.

We are:

    A rapid expanding international IT company.

    Based in the UK and USA, with 500 employees worldwide.

We want to:

    Recruit(招聘)staff for our office in Hangzhou.

    Recruit 30 staff members in the first year.

You should be:

    Chinese;

    A college graduate, majoring in Computer Science;

    Flexible, efficient, active;

    Willing to work in Hangzhou;

    Able to work unusual hours, e.g. 7 p.m. to 3 a.m.

You should have:

    Good basic English language skills, holding Level-A Certificate of Practical English Test for Colleges (PRETCO).

    Keyboard skills.

Way to contact us:

    0571-88044066

    For more details about the job, please visit our website: www.aaaltd.cn

A Job Advertisement

Recruitment: staff to work in an operations centre

Work place: ___1___

Unit 6　Technology and Life

Qualifications:
  Education: college graduate majoring in ___2___
  Foreign language: English, with Level-A Certificate of PRETCO
  Personal qualities: flexible, ___3___, active
  Working hours: ___4___, e.g. 7 p.m. to 3 a.m.
Way to get details about the job:
  Visit the website: ___5___

Task 4

Directions*: Complete the answers that follow the questions in no more than 3 words.*

Dear guests,

In order to serve you better, we are carrying out a reconstruction program at the hotel, which will improve our fitness facility.

We are currently work on our program on the 6th floor. We regret that the tennis court is not in operation.

However, you are still welcome to use the swimming pool. Please change into your swimsuit in your room.

While this program is in progress, drilling work may create some noise during the followingtime schedule:

9:00 a.m. to 11:00 a.m.

4:00 p.m. to 6:00 p.m.

We apologize for the inconvenience. Should you require any help during your stay with us, please call our Assistant Manager. He will be at your service any time of the day and night at 6120.

Once again, thank you for your kind understanding and have a pleasant stay!

Yours faithfully,
Arthur White
General Manager

1. What's the purpose of the hotel's reconstruction program?
   To improve its _____.
2. Where is the reconstruction work going in at the moment?

On the _____.

3. Where should guests change into their swimsuits before doing swimming?

   In their _____.

4. Why does the hotel apologize to the guests?

   Because of _____ caused by the reconstruction program.

5. Who should the guests turn to if they have any problem?

   They should call the _____.

Part Ⅴ Translation

Directions: *This part is to test your ability to translate English into Chinese. Make the best choice and write the translation of the paragraph.*

1. I will give you a clear idea of the market conditions in the region as soon as possible.

   A. 我会尽快让你们清楚地了解该地区的市场情况。

   B. 我将尽可能设法弄清楚该地区的市场销售状况。

   C. 我会尽早向你们清楚地说明该地区的市场状况。

   D. 我将尽可能地对该地区市场状况提出明确的想法。

2. One more assistant will be required to check reporter's names when they arrive at the press conference.

   A. 还需要一位助手在记者到达新闻发布会时核查他们的姓名。

   B. 还需要一位助手在记者到达新闻发布会时登记他们的姓名。

   C. 还有一位助手在到达新闻发布会时请记者通报他们的姓名。

   D. 还有一位助手要记者在到达新闻发布会时通报他们的姓名。

3. Mr. Smith has cancelled his trip because an urgent matter has come up which requires his immediate attention.

   A. 史密斯先生推迟了旅行,因为发生了一件大家都十分关注的紧急事件。

   B. 史密斯先生取消了旅行,因为发生了一件紧急的事情需要他立即处理。

   C. 史密斯先生取消了旅行,因为有一件棘手的事情需要他予以密切关注。

   D. 史密斯先生推迟了旅行,因为要处理一桩已引起公众关注的突发事件。

Unit 6 Technology and Life

4. The library is trying in every possible way to raise more money to meet its increasing running costs.

   A. 这个图书馆正尽一切努力增加更多收入以满足不断增长的日常开支。

   B. 这个图书馆正想尽一切办法提高收费标准并不断降低经营管理成本。

   C. 这个图书馆正尝试用各种办法提高收费标准以便尽早收回投资成本。

   D. 这个图书馆正想尽一切办法筹措更多资金满足越来越多的日常开支。

5. So, if we have to conclude as how technology has changed our lives, then the answer is that it has given us the power to make a difference in our lives by using it wisely. It depends on us, how we use and benefit from it, without getting addicted.

Part Ⅵ Writing

Directions: *With easier access to computer and the Internet, more and more college students turn to online courses and materials in their daily studies. Some even claim that online learning will replace classroom teaching. What is your opinion?*

Will Online Learning Replace Classroom Teaching?

1. 你是否支持用在线学习代替课堂教学;
2. 摆出论点和论据;
3. 总结。

Unit 7   Elite Entrepreneurs

Part I   Listening Comprehension

Section A

Directions: *There are 5 recorded questions in it. After each question, there is a pause. The questions will be spoken two times. When you hear a question, you should decide on the correct answer from the 4 choices marked A, B, C and D.*

1. A. Fine, thank you.   B. That's OK.
   C. Yes, that's right.   D. Here you are.
2. A. 5 grams.   B. 7 meters.
   C. 6 types.   D. 9 percent.
3. A. That's all right.   B. Not too bad.
   C. Yes, I'd like to.   D. Don't mention it.
4. A. Yes, she is.   B. No, she doesn't.
   C. Yes, she will.   D. No, she can't.
5. A. Hold on, please.   B. Speaking, please.
   C. Who are you?   D. Oh, I am the person.

Unit 7　Elite Entrepreneurs

Section B

Directions: *There are 5 recorded dialogues in it. After each dialogue, there is a recorded question. The dialogues and questions will be spoken only once. When you hear a question, you should decide on the correct answer from the 4 choices marked A, B, C and D.*

1. A. She is having a meeting now.　B. She is seeing a film then.
   C. She is meeting Mr Green now.　D. She is afraid of meeting the man.
2. A. Tuesday.　B. Thursday.　C. Wednesday.　D. Friday.
3. A. Very exciting.　　　　B. Rather boring.
   C. Quite interesting.　　D. Disappointing.
4. A. In a hospital.　　B. In a store.
   C. In a restaurant.　D. In a bank.
5. A. He is planning to buy a car.
   B. He is going to keep his old car.
   C. He has not enough money for a new car.
   D. He is afraid of buying a car.

Section C

Directions: *In this section you will hear a recorded short passage. The passage will be read three times. During the second reading, you are required to fill in the missing words or phrases according to what you hear. The third reading is for you to check your writing. Now the passage will begin.*

About the year 1900, a dart-haired boy named Charlie Chaplin was often seen waiting outside the back ___1___ of London theatres. He looked thin and hurry. He was hoping to get work in ___2___. He could sing and dance, and above all, he knew how to make people laugh. But he couldn't get work and therefore wandered about the city streets. Sometimes he was sent away to a home for children who had no parents.

But twenty years later, this same Chaplin became the greatest, ___3___, and best-loved comedian in the world. Any regular visitor to the cinema must have seen some of Charlie Chaplin's films. People everywhere have sat and laughed at them until the tears ___4___ their faces. Chaplin's comedy doesn't depend on words or language. It depends on   5   which mean the same thing to people all over the world.

Part II Dialogue

Section A

Directions: *Complete the following conversation by making the best choice in the table below.*

John: Congratulate you on graduating from BeijingUniversity.

Mike: Thank you!

John: Mike, at the moment, can you tell me your feelings?

Mike: _____

John: Do you enjoy your university life?

Mike: Yes, very much. I'll never forget the time in the university.

John: Really? _____

Mike: Thanks for my teachers, my classmates, my parents and all the people around me.

John: Your teachers are very kind to you all, aren't they?

Mike: Yes, _____, sometimes it seemed to be a little severe.

John: _____

Mike: And they are all well-informed.

Mike: _____

John: Yes, except that my classmates are always giving me their hands in my study. _____

John: Thank you for your time. _____

A. They're very strict with us
B. I can't express my feelings of thanks to them all.
C. Very excited and happy.
D. I think it is very helpful to you all.
E. Best wishes for you.
F. What do you want to say best?
G. You are so lucky!

Unit 7　Elite Entrepreneurs

Section B

Directions: *The following are the expressions about some situations. Read the words spoken and then match them with the functions.*

A. Have my bicycle been repaired yet? (　　)

B. Let's go home now. (　　)

C. Look! It's going to rain. (　　)

D. I'm sorry. I can't remember. (　　)

E. Have you got any small change? (　　)

F. I think you'd better see a doctor. (　　)

G. I'm sorry about that. (　　)

H. Congratulations! You are so great! (　　)

I. It's so noisy! I'm afraid I can't hear you. (　　)

1. Pointing to the cloud and telling your friend it's going to rain.

2. You haven't got any small change to buy a newspaper. Asking your friend for small change.

3. Suggesting your friend who has a flu should see a doctor.

4. Apologizing that you have made a mistake in a job.

5. Expressing your feelings that you couldn't hear what your friend said.

6. Asking someone if they have been repaired your broken bicycle that you left at a shop?

7. Apologizing to your friend that you can't remember the date of his birthday.

8. Congratulating on your friend who has passed the exam.

9. It's too late. Suggesting that you and your friend should go home.

Part Ⅲ　Vocabulary & Structure

Section A

Directions: *Complete each statement by choosing the appropriate answer from the 4 choices marked A, B, C and D.*

1. Many economists worried that overheating development might have a bad

_____ on the national economy in China.

　　A. cause　　　B. result　　　C. factor　　　D. effect

2. You may as well go outing all by yourself _____, I may keep you company.

　　A. differently　B. alternatively　C. accordingly　D. automatically

3. Professor Robison is now an expert in this field. It is years of hard work _____ has made him what he is today.

　　A. that　　　B. which　　　C. when　　　D. what

4. Yu Qiuyu is famous _____ a great writer _____ his great works.

　　A. for; as　　B. to; for　　C. as; for　　D. with; as

5. With the development of high technology, the Internet has _____ great changes to the way we work and think.

　　A. brought out　B. brought about　C. brought back　D. brought up

6. Online learning is being widely _____ to help adults further their education.

　　A. attended　　B. adopted　　C. adapted　　D. adjusted

7. The number of the students who _____ admitted into key universities _____ on the increase.

　　A. has been; is　　　　B. has been; are
　　C. have been; is　　　　D. have been; are

8. The company promised to pay some money for the customers _____ their shoddy goods and _____ an apology in public.

　　A. purchasing; making　　B. purchasing; make
　　C. purchased; to make　　D. to purchase; made

9. But for my friend's help, our team _____ the game last evening.

　　A. can lose　　B. will lose　　C. had lost　　D. would have lost

10. Taobao is Asia's largest retail network platform, _____ people can buy and sell many kinds of things.

　　A. where　　B. when　　C. that　　D. whose

Section B

Directions: *There are 10 incomplete statements here. You should fill each blank*

Unit 7 Elite Entrepreneurs

with the proper form of the word given in brackets.

1. When was the steam engine _____ (*invention*).
2. There are many _____ (*efficiency*)! methods of teaching.
3. The _____ (*operate*) of a new machine can be hard to learn.
4. The _____ (*apply*) of high technical knowledge makes daily life and work easy to perform.
5. I saw in the newspaper a teaching position _____ (*advertise*).
6. The two sides were unable to reach _____ (*agree*).
7. Nobody _____ (*allow*) to have the privilege to enter this museum.
8. They are very _____ (*consciousness*) of the problems involved.
9. She is an _____ (*experience*) traveller.
10. The work was assigned to them according to their _____ (*respect*) abilities.

Part Ⅳ Reading Comprehension

Task 1

Directions*: Read the following passage and make the correct choice.*

Since the Internet has come into homes, the daily life has never been the same again. But the thing that worries most of us is that we can get viruses from the internet. But can we catch viruses on our cell phones? A new study in the journey science says yes, but the spread of such mobile software that can bring harm to our cell phones won't reach dangerous levels until more cell phones are one the same operating system.

Computers are easily attacked by viruses because they share data, especially over the Internet. Of course, nowadays, more people are using their cell phones more and more frequently. They use them for emailing, text messaging and downloading troublesome ring tones, etc. So it is obvious are a threat, as well.

Scientists used nameless call data from more than six million cell phone users to help model a possible outbreak. And they concluded that viruses that spread from phone to phone by Bluetooth are not much concerned, because users have to be in close physical relation for their phones to "see" one another. However, viruses that spread through multimedia messaging services can move much faster, because they can come in disguise, such as a cool tune sent by a friend. The good news is that to be effective, these viruses need their victims to all use the same operating system, which not enough of us do. Because there is no Microsoft operating system for mobile phones yet. Thank goodness.

1. What's the passage mainly about?

    A. The operating system of cell phones.

    B. The threat of cell phone viruses.

    C. The wide use of cell phones.

    D. Computer viruses.

2. When _____, cell phone viruses can be dangerous.

    A. all the cell phones work on the same operating system

    B. Microsoft operating system for cell phones is created

    C. users can see each other on the phone

    D. Bluetooth is widely used

3. What can we infer about Bluetooth according to the scientists?

    A. It can increase the chances of cell phone viruses greatly.

    B. It can help us to stop the spreading of cell phone virtuses.

    C. It won't possibly cause the outbreak of cell phone viruses.

    D. It can make users have close physical relation with one another.

4. We can learn from the passage that _____.

    A. it is impossible to catch viruses on our cell phones

    B. cell phones are not well connected with the Internet

    C. it is dangerous for people to download ring tones to cell phones

    D. more than one operating system is available for cell phone users now

Task 2

Directions: *The following is a list of terms frequently used in business. After reading it, you are required to find the items equivalent to（与……等*

Unit 7 Elite Entrepreneurs

同) *those given in Chinese in the table below.*

A — distribution channels	B — sales agent
C — credit limit	D — assembly line
E — joint venture	F — subsidiary company
G — purchase price	H — advertising agent
I — full payment	J — board of directors
K — minimum price	L — operations management
M — retail price	N — feasibility reports
O — inner packing	P — make appointments
Q — quality specification	

Example：(O) 内包装　　　(E) 合资企业

1. ( ) 董事会　　　　　　( ) 广告代理商
2. ( ) 质量标准　　　　　( ) 可行性报告
3. ( ) 进货价格　　　　　( ) 零售价
4. ( ) 流水线　　　　　　( ) 生产管理
5. ( ) 销售渠道　　　　　( ) 最低价格

Task 3

Directions：*Complete the information by filling in the blanks. Write your answers in no more than 3 words.*

Business Memo

The business memo is probably the most frequently used communication within a company. It is called an intra-company communication because it is used by people in their own company or organization. They change to letters, however, when they write message to people who do not work for their company.

A memo creates a written record that may or may not be filed, depending on the receiver and the subject. As you know, spoken messages may be misunderstood or forgotten. A memo, however becomes a record that does much to ensure the complete communication between the sender and the receiver.

The standard form of a memo frequently carries a pre-printed series of items: To, From, Date, and Subject. The first two items include the names of the receiver and the sender. A well-written subject line tells the reader the key topic or topics the memo is about.

Business Memo

Frequent use: for communication within ___1___

Disadvantages of spoken messages:

They may be:

1. ___2___
2. ___3___

Contents of a memo:

1. Receiver.
2. ___4___
3. Date.
4. ___5___

Task 4

Directions: *Complete the answers that follow the questions in no more than 3 words.*

Nissan is truly a company in motion, one of the largest automakers in the world. You know Nissan by the Datsun cars and trucks they've built. Nissan. A company constantly striving to be better, faster, first. A company whose technology goes way beyond transportation. In the United States, we call it "Major Motion". Nissan has always been performance oriented. This is evidenced by the creation and development of the awesome Z car: A sports car that began a racing heritage second to none.

Yet Nissan is no stranger to economy. The economical and efficient Sentra quickly become American's leading import.

Unit 7 Elite Entrepreneurs

Nissan is also the company that redefined that trucking by inventing the compact truck and perfecting the King Cab. But rather than rest on its laurels, Nissan is always moving, always progressing, constantly improving. Today Nissan technology is at work developing new, even more effective power sources, pollution-free fuels, hybrid engines and electronic cars. Now, for uniformity worldwide. Nissan has changed the names of all its cars and trucks. Know in the United States as Dstsun, they will now bear the name of the parent company, Nissan. Nissan: a worldwide automotive company that takes motion to its final evolution. That's why everyone in America now has choice between just transport or the thrill of "Major Motion".

The message has been brought to you by Nissan Motor Corporation in USA, authorized distributor for Nissan Ltd., Japan.

The People Who have Made a Science of Motion for 50 Years.

1. In which country do we call it "Major Motion"?
   _____.

2. Why the Datsun cars and trucks are mentioned here?
   They are closely related to the car _____, frequently mentioned in this advertisement.

3. Why does Sentra quickly become American's leading import?
   Because it is _____.

4. What is at work developing new, even more effective power sources?
   _____.

5. By which company has the message been brought to you?
   _____.

Part V Translation

***Directions**: This part is to test your ability to translate English into Chinese. Make the best choice and write the translation of the paragraph.*

1. If I ordered a coat now, how long would it take before I get the delivery?
   A. 如果我现在就把外衣穿好,要多久我就能到达?

B. 如果我现在就把外衣的样品定好,要多久它才能交付?

C. 如果我现在订一件外衣,要多久才能把它做好?

D. 如果我现在订一件外衣,要多久才能接到货?

2. The government is introducing new production management standards for the food industry.

A. 政府正在介绍食品行业的新的生产管理标准。

B. 政府正在为食品行业介绍新的生产管理标准。

C. 政府正在为食品行业制定新的生产管理标准。

D. 政府正在引进新的代表食品行业的生产管理标准。

3. If they want to make any changes, we can make minor alternations of the project then.

A. 如果他们要作些改动的话,我们还可以对计划稍加修改。

B. 如果他们要求做任何改变,可以对项目做一些小的让步。

C. 如果他们要求做任何修改,那么可以把项目改得简单些。

D. 如果他们要做出任何变化,那么计划就能够得到改善。

4. Work gives us knowledge while play gives us rest. They are both necessary to us.

A. 工作给予我们知识,游玩给予我们休息,他们两者对我们都是必要的。

B. 工作和游玩既提供我们知识,又让我们有闲暇,他们两者对我们都是需要的。

C. 干活和游玩对我们都有益处,它使我们既能有本领,也能生活得悠闲。

D. 劳作与休闲对我们是必须的,一方面我们学到本事,另一方面我们还能休息。

5. We have everything college students need to know about GM's Cooperative Education and Intern Programs in our StudentCenter. For full-time college students, General Motors offers both a Cooperative Educationand an Intern Program. Participants in these real-business-world educational programs gain valuable degree-related experience, develop an insider's understanding of how GM works and earn competitive wages.

Part Ⅵ Writing

Directions: *This part is to test your ability to do practical writing. You are allowed 30 minutes to write a short passage. You should write at least 120 words according to the suggestion given below in Chinese.*

苹果公司将在未来推出 iPhone 新品

据国外媒体报道,苹果公司向媒体发出了新品发布会邀请函,确认新品发布会将在苹果 Cupertino 总部举行,并注明活动主题是"Let's talk iPhone"。根据以上材料,写一篇英语短文,但不能翻译材料。

Unit 8 Failure and Success

Part I Listening Comprehension

Section A

Directions: *There are 5 recorded questions in it. After each question, there is a pause. The questions will be spoken two times. When you hear a question, you should decide on the correct answer from the 4 choices marked A, B, C and D.*

1. A. Nice to meet you, Jack.   B. Hi, Jack.
   C. No, Jack.   D. Sure, Jack.
2. A. Great.   B. It's a pleasure.
   C. Let me try.   D. So do I.
3. A. $15.   B. 15 grams.
   C. Size 15.   D. 15 meters.
4. A. No, I didn't.   B. It was a waste of time.
   C. Yes, I did.   D. It lasted two hours.
5. A. That's OK.   B. I'm sorry.
   C. Impossible.   D. No way.

Unit 8 Failure and Success

Section B

Directions: *There are 5 recorded dialogues in it. After each dialogue, there is a recorded question. The dialogues and questions will be spoken only once. When you hear a question, you should decide on the correct answer from the 4 choices marked A, B, C and D.*

1. A. At a restaurant.   B. In a library.
   C. In a store.   D. In a post office.
2. A. £24.   B. £12.
   C. £15.   D. £20.
3. A. He is sick.   B. He is confident.
   C. He is well again.   D. He is worried.
4. A. Hotel manager and customer.   B. Boss and secretary.
   C. Customer and saleswoman.   D. Patient and doctor.
5. A. He missed his home.   B. He wanted to leave.
   C. He changed his job.   D. He was fired.

Section C

Directions: *In this section you will hear a recorded short passage. The passage will be read three times. During the second reading, you are required to fill in the missing words or phrases according to what you hear. The third reading is for you to check your writing. Now the passage will begin.*

All jobs create some type of stress. Perhaps your boss asks you to work ___1___ to complete a report by a certain ___2___. Perhaps it is ___3___ for you stand in the same spot at an assembly line eight hours a day, five days a week. Perhaps there are days when you are forced to sit at your desk with nothing to do, watching the clock, but you must not ___4___ because you are "at work". Each of these ___5___ creates stress.

Part Ⅱ　Dialogue

Section A

Directions: *Complete the following conversation by making the best choice in the table below.*

John: Hi, Mike. _____.

Mike: Hi. Are you mailing letters?

John: No. I'm here to cash my money order. _____?

Mike: I'm collecting a parcel.

John: From China?

Mike: Yes, from my parents. You see, my birthday is coming.

John: So there must be birthday gifts in the parcel.

Mike: _____. Will you come to my birthday party at the weekend?

John: _____. I'll bring you a special gift then.

Mike: _____.

John: With pleasure.

A. My pleasure.
B. I guess so.
C. That's very kind of you.
D. Nice to see you here.
E. What about you?
F. How is everything?
G. Good idea.

Section B

Directions: *The following are some expressions often used by people when they are talking about success or failure. Read the words spoken and then match*

Unit 8 Failure and Success

them with the functions.

A. You'll get it soon. (　)

B. That's the way it goes. (　)

C. I've already lost my heart. (　)

D. I wish you success. (　)

E. Congratulations on your promotion! (　)

F. Are you serious? (　)

G. Really outstanding job! (　)

H. I'm on top of the world. (　)

I. If there's anything you need, I won't be far away. (　)

1. Expressing depression.
2. Sending good wishes.
3. Offering your hand.
4. Expressing disbelief.
5. Giving encouragement.
6. Giving praise to someone.
7. Giving comfort.
8. Expressing excitement.
9. Extending congratulations.

Part Ⅲ　Vocabulary & Structure

Section A

***Directions**: Complete each statement by choosing the appropriate answer from the 4 choices marked A, B, C and D.*

1. The teacher was _____ she could train the boy to be a good student.

　　A. confident　　B. certain　　C. positive　　D. convince

2. Fatherhood was a new _____ for the careless young man.

　　A. work　　B. experience　　C. career　　D. pain

3. None can leave the building _____ they are required to do so.

A. if   B. unless   C. until   D. when

4. The little girl always wants to be the _____ of attention in a party.

   A. focus   B. center   C. heart   D. stress

5. You should pay more attention to what he meant _____ what he said.

   A. instead   B. otherwise   C. than   D. rather than

6. The secretary must get everything _____ before the important conference begins.

   A. good   B. well   C. complete   D. ready

7. He thinks he's _____ to us because his father's an important man.

   A. better   B. superior   C. bigger   D. greater

8. The young man was _____ as a fellow without principles.

   A. thought   B. saw   C. regarded   D. considered

9. I would appreciate _____ it a secret.

   A. your keeping   B. you to keep   C. that you keep   D. that you will keep

10. He was the most _____ of the people who've asked for the job.

    A. alike   B. likely   C. uniform   D. equivalent

Section B

Directions: *There are 10 incomplete statements here. You should fill each blank with the proper form of the word given in brackets.*

1. I am not completely _____ (*convince*) he understood the gravity of the situation.

2. It's a _____ (*romance*) film.

3. The public have lost _____ (*faithful*) in what the government is doing.

4. I tried to follow her _____ (*instruct*), but I got confused.

5. This is not how you _____ (*behavior*) towards a child.

6. For many childless couples, _____ (*adopt*) is the best solution.

7. This scheme will certainly make a _____ (*differ*) to the way I do my job.

8. Such a war could result in the use of chemical and _____ (*biology*) weapons.

9. Painting is a _____ (*creation*) process.

10. She made me feel stupid and _____ (*capable*).

Unit 8 Failure and Success

Part Ⅳ Reading Comprehension

Task 1

Directions: *Read the following passage and make the correct choice.*

  The eight airlines of the One World Alliance (联盟) have joined forces to give world travelers a simple way to plan and book a round-the-world journey. It's called the One World Explorer program.

  One world Explorer is the perfect solution for a once-in-a-lifetime holiday or an extended business trip. It's a great way for you to explore the four corners of the earth in the safe hands of the eight One World airlines.

  You can have hundreds of destinations to choose from, because the One World network covers the globe. And, as you travel around the world, you'll have the support of 260,000 people from all our airlines, who are devoted to the success of your journey, helping you make smooth transfers and offering support all along the way.

  The One World goal is to make global travel easier and more rewarding for every one of our travelers. We try our best to make you feel at home, no matter how far from home your journey may take you.

  We can offer travelers benefits on a scale beyond the reach of our individual networks. You'll find more people and more information to guide you at every stage of your trip, making transfers smoother and global travel less of a challenge.

  1. One World in the passage refers to _____.
     A. a travel agency
     B. a union of airlines
     C. a series of tourist attractions
     D. the title of a flight program

  2. The One World Explorer program is said to be most suitable for those who _____.
     A. have been to the four corners of the earth
     B. travel around the world on business

C. want to explore the eight airlines

  D. need support all along the way

3. The advantage of the alliance lies in _____.

  A. its detailed travel information

  B. its unique booking system

  C. its longest business flights

  D. its global service network

4. We can learn from the last paragraph that One World _____.

  A. offers the lowest prices to its passengers

  B. keeps passengers better informed of its operations

  C. offers better services than any of its member airlines alone

  D. is intended to make round-the-world trips more challenging

5. The purpose of the advertisement is to _____.

  A. promote a special flight program

  B. recommend long distance flights

  C. introduce different flight

  D. describe an airline group

Task 2

Directions: *The following is the contents of a book named Public Relations. After reading it, you are required to find the items equivalent to those given in Chinese in the table below.*

  A — Research and Analysis   B — Role of Departments

  C — Communication Process   D — Sampling Public Opinion

  E — Dealing with the News Media   F — Planning Actions

  G — Reaching the Audience   H — Opportunities in the Print Media

  I — Feedback and Evaluation   J — Public Opinion and Persuasion

  K — Social and Cultural Agencies L — Entertainment and Sports

  M — Government and Public Affairs N — Membership Organizations

  O — Legal Problems   P — International Public Relations

Unit 8 Failure and Success

Examples:（E）与新闻媒体打交道　　　（F）行动计划

```
1. (    ) 交流过程              (    ) 娱乐和体育
2. (    ) 国际公共关系          (    ) 公众意见抽样调查
3. (    ) 政府和公众事务        (    ) 研究与分析
4. (    ) 部门职能              (    ) 社会与文化机构
5. (    ) 反馈与评价            (    ) 法律问题
```

Task 3

Directions: *The following is a brief introduction on Macquarie University. After reading it, you are required to complete the outline below it briefly in no more than 3 words.*

Macquarie university is a major metropolitan（大都市的）university located in Sydney, Australia, with more than 20,000 students. Macquarie offers a broad range of high quality and contemporary courses in business, science, technology, law humanities and education.

Macquarie has a reputation as a research university with nine national research centers on campus and is committed to the link between teaching and research. The 135-hectare Macquarie campus at North Ryde provides an excellent learning environment for students just 16 kilometers north-west (20minutes by car) from Sydney's central business district. Macquarie is close to the M2 toll way and has public transport links to the rest of Sydney. The campus is modern, attractive, safe and spacious, with on-campus parking for private vehicles.

Staff are highly qualified, many of whom are leaders in their field. In recent years, Macquarie has become an international university offering management, business and applied finance courses in Singapore, Hong Kong and Japan. Macquarie University's global activities are being actively pursued through the development of courses using modern communications technology.

1. MacquarieUniversity is famous as a __1__ one.
2. If students in MacquarieUniversity go shopping, they had better go __2__ to the central business district.
3. __3__ cars can find parking area in Macquarie University.
4. Staff in Macquarie University are of high __4__.
5. As an __5__ university, Macquarie offers management, business and applied finance courses in Singapore, Hong Kong and Japan.

Task 4

Directions: *There is a letter below. After reading it you should give brief answer to the 5 questions in no more than 3 words.*

Dears Sirs,

Today we have received your bill for 150 name-bearing crystal vases which you sent us the other day.

We had ordered these vases on condition that they should reach us by the end of June. But they arrived here 15 days behind the schedule.

The customers refused to accept the goods because they arrived too late. Since the vases bear their names, we cannot sell them to other customers. So we asked the customers again and again to take the vases, and finally they agreed to accept them, but at a price cut of 30%.

You may understand how we have lost the customer's confidence in us. In this situation, we have to ask you to compensate for the loss we have suffered. We are looking forward to hearing from you soon.

Yours faithfully,
David Li

1. What was the problem with the delivery of the vases?
   They arrived 15 days _____.
2. When did the vases actually arrive?
   In the middle of _____.
3. Why couldn't the vases be sold to other customers?

Unit 8　Failure and Success

Because they were bearing _____ of those who ordered the vases.

4. In what condition did the customers accept the goods?

   At a price cut of _____.

5. What was the purpose of this letter?

   To ask the supplier to _____ for the loss they have suffered.

Part Ⅴ　Translation

Directions: *This part is to test your ability to translate English into Chinese. Make the best choice and write the translation of the paragraph.*

1. Once you gain confidence in yourself, you can judge truth and error with your own mind.

   A. 你万一获得了自信心,就能用自己的头脑判断真理和谬误。

   B. 你一旦对自己有了信心,就能用自己的心去判断正确和谬误。

   C. 一旦你获得了自信,你就能用自己的大脑评价真理和谬误。

   D. 一旦你有信心,你就用心灵来判断真理和谬误。

2. If the computer has finished the computations, a signal will be given at once.

   A. 如果计算机一算完,它就会立即给出信号。

   B. 一旦计算机完成运算,信号就会被立即给出。

   C. 如果计算机完成计算,它就会立即发出信号。

   D. 如果计算机被完成,人们就会发出信号。

3. Traditionally, it is believed that a successful system is one where you have the smallest class sizes, the largest number of teachers and the most money being spent.

   A. 传统相信好的教育体系是班级小,师资雄厚,资金投入多。

   B. 传统的人们认为成功的体系就是班级最小,教师最多,投入的钱最多。

   C. 传统观念认为成功的教育体系是班级小,师资雄厚,资金投入多。

   D. 从传统上说,班级最小,教师最多,投入的钱最多的教育体系是成功的。

4. If we had known the basic principles, we should have controlled the process even better.

A. 如果我们认识这些基本理论,我们就能更好地控制这个程序了。
B. 假如我们了解这些基本原理,我们应该早点控制这个过程。
C. 如果我们见过这些基本原理,那么我们必须更早一点控制这个程序的使用。
D. 如果我们早知道这些基本原理,我们就会更好地控制这个程序了。

5. Sometimes life hits you in the head with a brick. Don't lose faith. I'm convinced that the only thing that kept me going was that I loved what I did. You've got to find what you love. And that is as true for your work as it is for your own personal life. Your work is going to fill a large part of your life, and the only way to be truly satisfied is to do what you believe is great work.

Part Ⅵ　Writing

Directions: *Write a memo of no less than 100 words according to the given information.*

公司发现最近存在两个突出的问题:(1) 有员工违反规定在办公室吸烟;(2) 员工私家车乱停乱放。请以人事部 Steve Green 的名义给全体员工写一个备忘录,就上述两个问题表明公司的态度,内容包括:

第一个问题:
- 出现的问题;
- 重申公司有关规定;
- 违者处罚;

第二个问题:
- 问题及影响;
- 强调须在停车场停车;
- 违者处罚。

答案及听力材料

Key to Unit 1

Part Ⅰ Listening Comprehension

Section A

1~5 ABDCB

Section B

1~5 BCADA

Section C

1. every year   2. lost   3. building   4. rain   5. grow crops

Part Ⅱ Dialogue

Section A

1~6 CDABFE

Section B

A—5   B—1   C—6   D—2   E—3   F—7   G—4

Part Ⅲ Vocabulary & Structure

Section A

1~5 BDDAB   6~10 CBCDA

Section B

1. named 2. attitude(s) 3. relax 4. apologize 5. winds up

6. being admitted 7. attempted 8. contribute 9. left (has left) 10. crash

Part Ⅳ　Reading Comprehension

Task 1

1~5 BDABC

Task 2

1. K, Q 2. B, H 3. R, N 4. O, G 5. E, M

Task 3

1. Students 2. student card 3. newspaper or magazines 4. be fined

5. The librarian

Task 4

1. Yanton Playingfield Committee 2. return in July 3. rolling and trimming

4. drive and use 5. Hugh Morris

Part Ⅴ　Translation

1. B-A-C-D 2. B-A-D-C 3. B-C-D-A 4. B-D-A-C

5. 新开的假日酒店为您的家人欢度周末或您的公务旅行提供所需的一切服务。假日酒店的位置便利，步行即可到达温泉和中心商业区。每间客房均备有冰箱、咖啡壶和吹风机。入住的客人可以使用酒店的游泳池，每天早上可享用免费的中西式早餐。

Part Ⅵ　Writing

Dear Tom,

　　Thank you very much for the dictionary you gave me yesterday. You are always so thoughtful. You know I want to have such a dictionary for a long time. This summer I will take part in a intensive course. I tried my best to buy this expensive dictionary. Your gift is on the time and when I use this dictionary, I will miss you.

Yours sincerely,

Mary

答案及听力材料部分

Script for Listening Comprehension

Part Ⅰ Listening Comprehension

Section A

1. Are you going to buy a house?
2. Have you read today's newspaper?
3. What time do you usually go to work?
4. Have you received my letter?
5. Do you often go shopping at weekends?

Section B

1. M: It's very cold this morning.
   W: You're right. It's much colder than yesterday.
   Q: What's the weather like this morning?

2. M: I'm going to Beijing tomorrow. Would you please book a ticket for me?
   W: Sure. With pleasure.
   Q: What will the woman probably do?

3. M: What do you think of your new boss?
   W: I don't like him. He is too serious.
   Q: What does the woman think of her new boss?

4. W: I'm afraid We'll be late for the party.
   M: Don't worry. There is still twenty minutes to go.
   Q: What does the man mean?

5. M: Is there anything I can do for you?
   W: Thank you very much. But I can do it all by my self.
   Q: What does the woman mean?

Section C

The world population today is about 6 billion. But only about 11 percent of the world's land is suitable for farming. However, the area of farmland is becoming smallerand smaller <u>every year</u>. So it will be difficult to feed so many mouths. There are several reasons why farmland is being <u>lost</u>. First, a lot of the land is being used for the building of houses. Secondly, some of the land has become wasteland because wind and rain have removed the top soil. Thirdly, some of the land has become too salty to grow crops.

Therefore, a big problem that we face today is hunger.

Part Ⅱ　Dialogue

Section A

1. I can't even remember the last time we made a profit.
2. I think it's time to face the problem.
3. I'll call the lawyer in the morning and tell her we are going under.
4. We ran out of money and had to close the store.
5. All you have to do is sign some papers.
6. Come anytime after two o'clock.

Key to Unit 2

Part Ⅰ　Listening Comprehension

Section A

1~5　CADAB

Section B

1~5　DDBCA

Section C

1. on business　2. safe　3. For example　4. helpful　5. always

Part Ⅱ　Dialogue

Section A

1~7　CEAFBD

Section B

A—4　B—5　C—1　D—7　E—3　F—6　G—2

Part Ⅲ　Vocabulary & Structure

Section A

1~5　DCBCC　6~10　BBABA

答案及听力材料部分

Section B

1. turned to 2. discouraged 3. on the way 4. apply 5. promising
6. explored 7. being admitted 8. acquainted with 9. appreciate 10. vary

Part Ⅳ Reading Comprehension

Task 1

1~5 CCDAB

Task 2

1. K,N 2. H,B 3. L,D 4. G,P 5. I,J

Task 3

1. 200 2. phone-card 3. put in 4. call 5. card-phone place

Task 4

1. the clock 2. cold area 3. Minute Timer 4. The support 5. will not run

Part Ⅴ Translation

1. A-C-D-B 2. A-B-C-D 3. C-A-B-D 4. A-B-C-D

5. 无论你网络的规模是大还是小,你知道计算机的价钱在使用计算机的总额费用中常常只占很小的一部分。而网络的管理和维护却可使费用增加并影响运行,为此,我们开发了一套工具软件,以帮助你使用和管理各种系统。

Part Ⅵ Writing

Basketball match

Team：Anhui University VS Anhui Normal University

Time：8:30 a.m.   4th Nov   (Thurs)

Place：playground

Please ask for tickets from students' Union. Fans will be sent to the place by 3 buses.

All fans should gather at the front of the library at 8 a.m.

Script for Listening Comprehension

Part Ⅰ Listening Comprehension

Section A

1. Excuse me, are you Mr. Smith from America?
2. Mr. Jonn, when is the library open?
3. It's rather hot today, would you please open the window?
4. What do you think of your boss?
5. What's the weather like in your city?

Section B

1. W: Are you coming for the basketball game?
   M: Yes, I've got a ticket from my brother.
   Q: Where did the man get the ticket'?

2. M: Can you stay for dinner?
   W: I'd love to, but I have to go to meet a friend at the airport.
   Q: What's the woman going to do?

3. W: I'm here to see Miss Brown.
   M: Miss Brown? Oh, she is in her office.
   Q: Where is Miss Brown?

4. M: Do you like your new job?
   W: Yes, I like it very much.
   Q: How does the woman feel about her new job?

5. W: Did you work as a salesman in that company?
   M: No, I was an engineer.
   Q: What did the man do in that company?

Section C

People visit other countries for many reasons. Some travel <u>on business</u>; others travel to visit interesting places. Whenever you go, for whatever reason, it is important to be <u>safe</u>. A tourist can draw a lot of attention from local people. Although most of the people you meet are friendly and welcoming, sometimes there are

答案及听力材料部分

dangers. <u>For example</u>, your money or passport might be stolen. Just as in your homecountry, do not expect everyone you meet to be friendly and <u>helpful</u>. It is important to prepare your trip in advance, and <u>always</u> be careful while you are traveling.

Part Ⅱ Dialogue

Section A

1. Tell me a little bit about yourself.
2. What kind of personality do you think you have?
3. I'm very organized and extremely capable.
4. I suppose my strengths are I'm persistent and a fast-learner.
5. Do you have any licenses or certificates?
6. I'm very co-operative and have good teamwork spirit.

Key to Unit 3

Part Ⅰ Listening Comprehension

Section A

1~5 DBDDD

Section B

1~5 CBDBD

Section C

1. Destroy 2. Surface 3. kilometers 4. was hit by 5. height

Part Ⅱ Dialogue

Section A

1~5 EDCBA

Section B

A—4 B—2 C—3 D—1

Part Ⅲ Vocabulary & Structure

Section A

1~5 AACDB 6~10 ADCDD

Section B

1. lonely 2. developed 3. presents 4. merge 5. announced

6. Slow down 7. instructions 8. available 9. book 10. forced

Part Ⅳ Reading Comprehension

Task 1

1～5 CBCAC

Task 2

1. J,M 2. A,D 3. N,G 4. F,O 5. K,L

Task 3

1. written permission 2. Submit 3. the Personnel Office

4. the following Monday 5. department manager

Task 4

1. correspondence 2. customers' needs 3. Supervisory experience

4. (An) attractive salary 5. four weeks / a month

Part Ⅴ Translation

1. D-B-A-C 2. A-B-D-C 3. C-A-D-B 4. D-C-B-A

5. 夏威夷地处热带,气候却温和宜人,年平均温度常年保持在24度左右。岛上时时刮过的东北风,伴着太平洋吹来的阵阵海风,让人倍感凉爽舒适。

Part Ⅵ Writing

Application Form

Family name:Wang   First name:Xiaoming

Date of Birth:20th,August 1989   Nationality:Han

Sex:Male   Telephone number:020-61006571

Address:No.710 Zhongshan Road,Guangzhou

Please write about your educational background and work experience, the university and the major you want to apply and the information you want to know. (about 50 words)

Since my graduation from Anhui Universty as an English major, I have been working as a translator for a few years. I'm very interested in "Chinese as Foreign Language" and I intend to apply for that major in your Universty. I will really appreciate your kindness if you can offer me the courses related to this major.

Script for Listening Comprehension

Part Ⅰ Listening Comprehension

Section A

1. What's the time now?
2. Why not have a cup of coffee together?
3. Can you hand this to me?
4. How long have you been in Beijing?
5. How are you feeling now?

Section B

1. M: I'd like to drive to the piano concert, but my brother will use the car tonight.

    W: Who needs a car? We can take the subway if we go a little earlier.

    Q: What does the woman suggest?

2. W: Can you tell me what time MU9173 Flight arrives?

    M: Yes, at 6:00 p.m., but it has been delayed for two hours.

    Q: When is the airplane now expected to arrive?

3. W: Have you been waiting for me for a long time?

    M: I've only been waiting for an hour. I feel as though I had been standing here for 20 days.

    Q: How long has the man been waiting for her?

4. W: Which color would you choose?

    M: It makes no difference to me.

    Q: What does the man say about the color?

5. W: Good morning, Hilton Hotel. May I help you?

    M: Hi, I'd like some information about your hotel.

    Q: What is the woman?

Section C

What do we know about sea? Most of us have seen it. Many of us have swum in it. We know that it looks very pretty when the sun is shining on it. And we also know that the sea is full of waves. Waves are beautiful to look at, but they can <u>destroy</u> ships at sea, as well as houses and buildings near the shore. What causes waves? Most waves are caused by winds blowing over the <u>surface</u> of the water. The sun heats the earth, causing the air to rise and the winds to blow. The winds blow across the sea, pushing little waves into enormous ones. When the wind is blowing at 120 <u>kilometers</u> per hour, most waves will be about 12 meters high. In 1993 the United States <u>was hit by</u> the largest measured wave in history. It rose in the Pacific Ocean to a <u>height</u> of 34 meters

Part Ⅱ   Dialogue

Section A

Tom: Hello, Lucy! I've lost my dictionary. Have you seen it anywhere?

Lucy: Sorry, I haven't. Why don't you ask Jim? Perhaps he's seen it.

Tom: Thanks, I will.

Lucy: Oh, here he is.

Tom: Jim, have you seen my dictionary?

Jim: Yes, I have. I saw it on Lin Tao's desk about five minutes ago. It must still be there.

Tom: Thanks very much.

Jim: You're welcome.

Key to Unit 4

Part Ⅰ   Listening Comprehension

Section A

1~5   CDDAC

Section B

1~5   DBCCA

答案及听力材料部分

Section C

1. Phenomenon   2. other than   3. United States   4. Reflects   5. such as

Part Ⅱ   Dialogue

Section A.

1. Great!   2. quantity discount   3. We sure do   4. place an order
5. Here is our price list

Section B

A—5   B—2   C—3   D—4   E—1

Part Ⅲ   Vocabulary & Structure

Section A

1~5   CACDB   6~10   CBBAB

Section B

1. permission   2. *nutritions*   3. *denied*   4. *icon*   5. invention
6. *reveals*   7. *removed*   8. *prompted*   9. *symbolized*   10. infection

Part Ⅳ   Reading Comprehension

Task 1

1~5   ADABC

Task 2

1. D,O   2. L,J   3. A,E   4. N,P   5. G,I

Task 3

1. tuition   2. return   3. pocket money   4. own educational career
5. February 1,2009

Task 4

1. Fourteen weeks   2. sales support activities
3. business communication skills   4. an online catalog   5. an interview

Part Ⅴ   Translation

1. B-D-A-C   2. A-D-C-B   3. C-B-D-A   4. D-B-A-C

5. 灵活工作制是20世纪60年代在德国出现的,1972年传到英国。这种制度允许工人在他们愿意的时间内开始和结束工作,只有两点要求。第一,所有工人必须在白天的"关键"时间里来上班。第二,所有工人每周必须干满应该工作的时间。

Part VI Writing(Only for reference)

Dear Sir or Madam,

We have seen the advertisement of your bicycles on television, and we are very interested in your machines for both men and women, and also for children. Would you please send us a copy of your catalog and current price list for bicycles?

We are the leading bicycle dealers in Wuhan, and have branches in ten neighboring districts. If the quality of your products is satisfactory and the price is reasonable, we will place regular orders for fairly large numbers.

We look forward to your reply!

Yours sincerely,

Wang Gang

Sales Manager

Script for Listening Comprehension

Part I Listening Comprehension

Section A

1. Where is your T-shirt?

2. Do you like the bread with some butter?

3. Where did he go for business trip?

4. How do you think of the party last night?

5. Is there any news in today's newspaper?

Section B

1. M: I find it so hard to use the new words in sentences.

   W: Don't give up. Rome was not built in one day.

   Q: What does the man want to do?

2. W: Sorry, the visiting time is over. Please come here to see your mother

答案及听力材料部分

tomorrow.

Q: What does the man want to do?

3. W: Please be quick. I will be late.

M: Don't worry. The film will be on at 6 o'clock, and it is still 30 mins left.

Q: What's the time now?

4. W: The bus has not arrived yet. What's wrong?

M: The bridge was collapsed and bus won't come until 9:15.

Q: When will the bus arrive?

5. W: The traffic is so busy. I could not come to office on time.

M: Don't worry, we are just 5mins late.

Q: How late are they now?

Section C

Since World War Two, especially in the last few decades of the 20th century, large groups of foreigners have come and settled in the United Sates. The <u>phenomenon</u> is that many Americans speak a foreign language at home. Today, one in seven Americans speaks a language <u>other than</u> English. Spanish is the leading foreign language spoken by 17 million Americans. All together, 31.8 million Americans speak 329 foreign languages in the <u>United States</u>. That means there is an increase of 34 percent in foreign language usage since 1980. Asia languages are used by 14 percent of foreign language speakers. That <u>reflects</u> the new wave of immigrants from Asia countries <u>such as</u> India, Japan, Korea and the Philippines. However, fewer European languages are heard in American families than before.

Part Ⅱ Dialogue

Section A

Leslie: How are you this afternoon?

Paul: Just fine. I looked over the catalog you gave me this morning, and I'd like to discuss prices on your computer speakers

Leslie: Very good. Great!

Paul: Let me see. I see that your listed price for the K-two-one model is ten US dollars. Do you offer a quantity discount?

Leslie: We sure do. We give a five percent discount for orders of a hundred or more.

Paul: What kind of discount could you give me if I were to place an orderfor six hundred units?

Leslie: On an order of six hundred, we can give you a discount of ten percent.

Paul: I'd like to go ahead and place an order for six hundred units.

Leslie: Here is our price list. I'll just fill out the purchase order and have you sign it.

Key to Unit 5

Part Ⅰ Listening Comprehension

Section A

1~5 CDBDC

Section B

1~5 DACDC

Section C

1. on business 2. safe 3. For example 4. helpful 5. be careful

Part Ⅱ Dialogue

Section A

1~5 DABEC

Section B

A—3 B—1 C—2 D—7 E—5 F—4 G—6

Part Ⅲ Vocabulary & Structure

Section A

1~5 ADAAC 6~10 DABBC

Section B

1. according 2. behavior 3. disgraceful 4. Environmentalists

5. increasingly 6. tointeract 7. operated 8. unprepared

9. romantic 10. connecting

答案及听力材料部分

Part Ⅳ Reading Comprehension

Task 1

1~5 DABAD

Task 2

1. L,N   2. D,J   3. E,H   4. K,M   5. I,G

Task 3

1. Tourist Information Centre   2. local events   3. coach companies

4. walking hours   5. guidebooks

Task 4

1. A tour guide   2. 2   3. The Petrified Forest   4. beautifully colored stone

5. petrified wood

Part Ⅴ Translation

1. A-C-D-B   2. A-D-B-C   3. D-A-B-C   4. A-C-D-B

5. 我们非常高兴地欢迎中国朋友参加本届商务专修培训项目。在这里，你们将参加丰富多彩的活动，并有机会进行互动交流。希望大家通过本培训项目获得巨大收益。培训期间，无论有什么样的问题或想法，请告诉我们，不要客气。我们相信本培训将既有教育意义又令大家愉快。

Part Ⅵ Writing

Dear Lily：

I am so glad to know that you will come to Hong Kong and visit us. Hong Kong is a great place for fun. I'm sure that you will enjoy yourself here.

Of course Hong Kong Disneyland is a must-see park where you can join the Parade and watch fireworks show which will transform the sky above Sleeping Beauty Castle into a stunning evening spectacle. You can also watch the shows like "Festival of the Lion King", "The Golden Mickeys" and "Stitch Encounter". Characters from cartoon films will appear occasionally at the park.

Although Disneyland is not a big park, you'll have to spend a day there so that you can experience all of the items. Don't forget to ask for a map of the park and a daily calendar of the shows so that you can arrange your time well.

I'm looking forward to your coming.

Yours sincerely,

Mary

Script for Listening Comprehension

Part I Listening Comprehension

Section A

1. How about the party last night?
2. Can I come and have a look at your new house?
3. Do you think you'll be able to go mountain-climbing tomorrow?
4. Have you finished it on time?
5. How could you be so rude as to walk in here in the middle of my class?

Section B

1. W: Welcome to China. Can I have your passport, customs and health declaration forms, please?
   M: OK. Here they are.
   Q: Where do you think the dialogue most probably take place?

2. W: Mr. Baker, may I know your occupation?
   M: Computer engineer at Motorola.
   Q: What's Mr. Baker's job?

3. M: I'm here on vacation, and you, Miss Wang?
   W: I'm teaching Chinese in a language school here.
   Q: What does Miss Wang do?

4. M: I have two tickets for the art exhibition this weekend. Would you like to come?
   W: Sure. I'd love to.
   Q: What are the speakers going to do this weekend?

5. M: I'd like something typically Chinese.
   W: Fine. We serve a wide range of typical Chinese food. Here is the menu.
   Q: What is the probable relationship between the speakers?

答案及听力材料部分

Section C

Hello, everybody! On behalf of the college, I'd like to express my warmest welcome to you. We do hope all our students will feel happy and pleasant here. We would be pleased to offer you all kinds of help to make your life here fruitful and colorful. Here you can find many convenient facilities for you to use, such as a student center, two libraries and an indoor playground. We also have four dinning halls serving Chinese food and Western foods. Any suggestions for improving our service are welcome. Thank you for your attention.

Part II Dialogue

Section A

W: Good morning. Can I help you?.

M: We'd like to buy some famous Chinese arts and crafts articles. What would you like to recommend?

W: There are various kinds of such articles in our shop, for example, porcelain, embroidery, cloisonné, wood engraving, and writing brush. May I show you around?

M: They're all marvelous! We'll buy one china tea set, one tri-colored pottery, one wood engraving, and three Chinese embroidery shirts. How much are they together?

W: Altogether 880 yuan. Let me wrap them up for you.

M: That's fine. Here is 900 yuan.

W: Here are the change and the receipt.

M: Thank you.

W: Wish you have a good time in China.

Key to Unit 6

Part I Listening Comprehension

Section A

1~5 ABCBD

Section B

1～5　DACDB

Section C

1. deal with　2. useful　3. effect　4. totally　5. wonderful

Part Ⅱ　Dialogue

Section A

1～5　BEADC

Section B

A—4　B—5　C—1　D—3　E—2

Part Ⅲ　Vocabulary & Structure

Section A

1～5　DCDBA　6～10　DDCAD

Section B

1. dominant　2. competing　3. present　4. integrity　5. beneficial

6. activity　7. addictive　8. circle　9. accountant　10. unite

Part Ⅳ　Reading Comprehension

Task 1

1～5　BABCB

Task 2

1. H,M　2. N,I　3. P,D　4. B,F　5. A,E

Task 3

1. Hangzhou

2. Computer Science

3. efficient

4. unusual hours

5. www. aaaltd. cn

Task 4

1. Fitness facilities　2. 6th floor　3. rooms　4. the inconvenience

答案及听力材料部分

5. Assistant Manager

Part Ⅴ Translation

1. A-C-B-D   2. A-B-D-C   3. B-C-D-A   4. D-A-C-B

5. 要是总结科技是如何改变我们生活的话,那就是通过聪明地使用它让我们的生活变得不同。这取决于我们怎么去使用它并从中受益,而不是对它上瘾。

Part Ⅵ Writing

Will Online Learning Replace Classroom Teaching?

Because of the rapid growth and various advantages of cyber education, many people have begun to dream of the dominance of on learning. However, while it is convenient and easy to take online lessons, I still think that classroom teaching should take the priority.

First of all, in the classroom, the teacher and students can carry on face-to-face and intimate communication, which benefits enormously. An active student can raise questions whenever he wants and the teacher can adjust his method of teaching by reading students' expressions.

Secondly, the classroom is a good place to build teamwork. While technologies may make some team discussions possible on the Internet, real teamwork can only be achieved in the classroom.

To conclude, in the classroom, people communicate better, have more fun, and develop teamwork. It can be said that classroom teaching is not only pleasant, but also fruitful and efficient. So I think online learning will not replace classroom teaching.

Script for Listening Comprehension

Part Ⅰ Listening Comprehension

Section A

1. Could you please send this letter for me?
2. When can I come to have my photos?

3. Excuse me, is that seat taken?

4. Would you please tell me something about the machines?

5. Mr. Wang, shall I take a message for you?

Section B

1. M: Hi, Alice. How is everything with you?

   W: As busy as usual.

   Q: What can we learn from the dialogue?

2. W: May I use the telephone?

   M: Sure, and the local calls are free.

   Q: What does the man say about the local calls?

3. M: Did you hear about the bus accident last night?

   W: Yes, it was terrible. Five people were injured.

   Q: What happened last night?

4. W: I'm going to the railway station. Can you drive me there?

   M: Yes, it's my pleasure.

   Q: What will the man do?

5. M: Shall we have the meeting at ten o'clock on Wednesday morning?

   W: Wednesday morning at ten? It's OK for me.

   Q: What are they talking about?

Section C

More technology has a big influence on our daily life. New devices are widely used today. For example, we have to deal with the Internet everyday. It is becoming more and more useful to nearly everybody. Now it's time to think about how the Internet influence us, what effect it has on our social behavior and what the future world will look like. The Internet has totally changed our life, there is no doubt about that. I think that the Internet has changed our life in a wonderful way.

Part Ⅱ Dialogue

Section A

Linda: Good morning! What can I do for you?

Jack: Yes, I want to borrow a book.

Linda: Have you got a library card?

Jack: No, I don't have one now. How can I get one?

Linda: Well, please fill in this form first.

Jack: OK. (A few minutes later.) Here's the completed form.

Linda: Thanks. The card will be ready in thirty minutes, and you can take it later.

Jack: Thank you. By the way, how long can I keep the book?

Linda: Well, two weeks. But then, you can renew the book if you still need it.

Jack: I see. Thanks a lot.

Linda: My pleasure.

Key to Unit 7

Part Ⅰ Listening Comprehension

Section A

1~5 CCBAA

Section B

1~5 CDACB

Section C

1) entrances   2) show business   3) best-known   4) ran down comedy

5) little actions

Part Ⅱ Dialogue

Section A

1~7 CFADGBE

Section B

A—6 B—9 C—1 D—7 E—2 F—3 G—4 H—8 I—5

Part Ⅲ Vocabulary & Structure

Section A

1~5 DBACB   6~10 BCBDA

Section B

1. invented 2. efficient 3. operation 4. application 5. advertised

6. agreement 7. is allowed 8. conscious 9. experienced 10. respectful

Part IV Reading Comprehension

Task 1

1~4 BACD

Task 2

1. J,H 2. Q,N 3. G,M 4. D,L 5. A,K

Task 3

1. a company 2. misunderstood 3. forgotten 4. Sender 5. Subject

Task 4

1. The Unite States 2. Nissan 3. economical and efficient

4. Nissan technology 5. Nissan Motor Corporation

Part V Translation

1. D-C-B-A 2. C-A-B-D 3. A-C-B-D 4. A-B-D-C

5. 我们学生中心有大学生需要了解的有关通用公司合作教育和实习项目的一切信息。对于脱产大学生，通用汽车公司既提供合作教育服务也提供实习服务。在这种实际商务的教育过程中，参与者能够获得与所学专业相关的宝贵经验，加深对通用汽车公司内部工作流程的了解并赚取可观的薪金。

Part VI Writing

One possible version：

The products of Apple Company are popular in the IT market in the world, such as the series of iPhones and the iPads. They get us to know something about more use of the mobile phone.

As the customers are eager to know what the Apple Company will put to the market, a piece of new information gets them excited. That is new type of iPhone will be put into the market in future. The theme of the new iPhone is "Let's talk iPhone". I think new iPhone will also be a great shock to the customers and iPhone lovers.

Script for Listening Comprehension

Part I Listening Comprehension

Section A

1. Excuse me, Is it your first time to Beijing?
2. How many different models of this motorcycle do you offer?
3. Hi, Jimmy! How are things going?
4. Your friend Rose is from London, isn't she?
5. May I speak to Mr Smith?

Section B

1. M: Can you come and see me at nine o'clock?
   W: I'm afraid not. I'm meeting Mr. Green at that time.
   Q: Why can't the woman go to see the film?

2. W: I would like to see Professor Smith as soon as possible.
   M: I'm sorry. The Professor Smith was ill on Monday. He'll probably be back on Friday, but I suggest you might call on Thursday to be sure.
   Q: When can the woman expect to see Professor Smith?

3. M: What do you think of this play?
   W: It's so exciting. I enjoyed every minute of it.
   Q: What does the woman think of the play?

4. W: What can I do for you, sir?
   M: I'd like some fried chicken and a packet of chips, please?.
   Q: Where does the conversation most probably take place?

5. M: Has Robert decided to buy a new car?
   W: Hardly, I am afraid he can't afford it.
   Q: What do we know about Robert?

Section C

About the year 1900, a dark-haired boy named Charlie Chaplin was often seen waiting outside the back entrances of London theatres. He looked thin and hurry. He was hoping to get work in show business. He could sing and dance, and above all, he knew how to make people laugh. But he couldn't get work and therefore wandered about the city streets. Sometimes he was sent away to a home for children who had no parents.

But twenty years later, this same Chaplin became the greatest, best-known, and best-loved comedian in the world. Any regular visitor to the cinema must have seen some of Charlie Chaplin's films. People everywhere have sat and laughed at them until the tears ran down their faces. Chaplin's comedy doesn't depend on words or language. It depends on little actions which mean the same thing to people all over the world.

Part II Dialogue

Section A

John: Congratulate you on graduating from Beijing University.

Mike: Thank you!

John: Mike, at the moment, can you tell me your feelings?

Mike: Very excited and happy.

John: Do you enjoy your university life?

Mike: Yes, very much. I'll never forget the time in the university.

John: Really? What do you want to say best?

Mike: Thanks for my teachers, my classmates, my parents and all the people around me.

John: Your teachers are very kind to you all, aren't they?

Mike: Yes, They're very strict with us, sometimes it seemed to be a little severe.

John: I think it is very helpful to you all.

Mike: And they are all well-informed.

Mike: You are so lucky!

John: Yes, except that my classmates are always giving me their hands in my study. I can't express my feelings of thanks to them all.

John: Thank you for your time. Best wishes for you.

答案及听力材料部分

Key to Unit 8

Part I Listening Comprehension

Section A

1~5 DCABA

Section B

1~5 BBCAD

Section C

1. overtime   2. deadline   3. necessary   4. leave   5. situations

Part II Dialogue

Section A

1. Nice to see you here.   2. What about you?   3. I guess so.
4. My pleasure.   5. That's very kind of you.

Section B

A—5 B—7 C—1 D—2 E—9 F—4 G—6 H—8 I—3

Part III Vocabulary & Structure

Section A

1~5 ABCAD   6~10 DBCAB

Section B

1. convinced   2. romantic   3. faith   4. instructions   5. behave
6. adoption   7. difference   8. biological   9. creative   10. incapable

Part IV Reading Comprehension

Task 1

1~5 BBDCA

Task 2

1. C,L   2. P,D   3. M,A   4. B,K   5. I,O

Task 3

1. research 2. south-east 3. Private 4. qualification 5. international

Task 4

1. behind the schedule 2. July 3. the names 4. 30% 5. compensate

Part V　Translation

1. C-D-B-A 2. C-A-B-D 3. C-D-B-A 4. D-B-A-C

5. 有些时候，生活会拿起一块砖头向你的脑袋上猛拍一下。不要失去信心。我很清楚唯一使我一直走下去的，就是我做的事情令我无比钟爱。你需要去找到你所爱的东西。对于工作是如此，对于你的个人生活也是如此。你的工作将会占据生活中很大的一部分。你只有相信自己所做的是伟大的工作，你才能怡然自得。

Part Ⅵ　Writing

June 30, 2012

To：All Members of Staff

From：Steve Green, Personnel Dept.

Re：Smoking and Car Parking

Smoking

Recently we have found that there are staff members smoking in the office. We would like to remind everyone that the office is a Non-Smoking area. Smoking in the office will do harm to all staff members. We confirm that smoking is restricted to the coffee lounge and the terrace or outside the office building. A fine will be issued on smokers.

Car Parking

For the past few weeks the company has got several complaints on the disorder of car parking. This may lead to serious result and have bad influence if there is an emergency in the office building. We would like to confirm that those who drive to work, please park your car behind the office building in the parking lot. A fine will be issued on those who do not park the car in the parking lot.

答案及听力材料部分

Script for Listening Comprehension

Part I Listening Comprehension

Section A

1. May I have your name, sir?
2. My recorder doesn't work. Could you fix it?
3. The flower looks nice. How much is it?
4. Hi, Tom. How did you like the movie you saw last night?
5. I'm sorry to have kept you waiting.

Section B

1. W: There are three books for one person.
   M: Fine. I'll be certain to return them on time.
   Q: Where did this conversation probably take place?

2. W: Can I buy two tickets to London for tonight?
   M: All right, 24 pounds, please.
   Q: How much is one ticket for London?

3. W: How did your interview go?
   M: I couldn't feel better about it!
   Q: How did the man feel about the interview?

4. W: Hello, I want to book a room which faces the sea.
   M: Hold the line please. I will find out.
   Q: What is the relationship between the two speakers?

5. W: John, why isn't Tom working here today?
   M: He was dismissed last month.
   Q: Why did Tom leave here?

Section C

All jobs create some type of stress. Perhaps your boss asks you to work <u>overtime</u> to complete a report by a certain <u>deadline</u>. Perhaps it is <u>necessary</u> for you to stand in the same spot at an assembly line eight hours a day, five days a week. Perhaps there are days when you are forced to sit at your desk with nothing to do, watching the clock, but you must not leave because you are "at work". Each of these situations creates stress.

Part II Dialogue

Section A

　　John: Hi, Mike. Nice to see you here.

　　Mike: Hi. Are you mailing letters?

　　John: No. I'm here to cash my money order. What about you?

　　Mike: I'm collecting a parcel.

　　John: From China?

　　Mike: Yes, from my parents. You see, my birthday is coming.

　　John: So there must be birthday gifts in the parcel.

　　Mike: I guess so. Will you come to my birthday party at the weekend?

　　John: My pleasure. I'll bring you a special gift then.

　　Mike: That's very kind of you.

　　John: With pleasure.